Time with God

Develop Confidence and Consistency in Your Personal Prayer Life

Kevin T. Cunningham

Time with God

Copyright © 2015 by KEVIN T. CUNNINGHAM

All Scripture paraphrases are those of the author unless otherwise noted. Information about all Scripture Translations Used is at the end of the book.

All rights reserved. No part of this publication may be reproduced, stored in a retrieval system, or transmitted by any means—electronic, mechanical, photographic (photocopying), recording, or otherwise—without prior permission in writing from the author.

Learn more information and access additional resources at www.TimeWithGodBook.com or www.EncourageAndEquip.com.

Dedication

This book is dedicated to all those who long to love God with their whole heart, mind, soul, and strength but still fight the distractions of our day, every day.

This is offered that God may use it to draw us closer to himself.

Endorsements

In *Time with God,* Kevin Cunningham takes a huge subject like prayer and creates an easy path to understand how to pray. We know we should pray. We know there is power in prayer. But, the how to of prayer is often elusive, especially because the enemy knows this is where the real Kingdom work is accomplished.

Time with God is the flesh on the bones of a spiritual discipline that we need to develop like a muscle. Mr. Cunningham creates doable exercises that help us to put words to our thoughts about God and the power of praying His will in all situations.

—Jeanne Doyon
Writer, Speaker & Teacher

This book with its outlines, Scripture paraphrases, and suggestions can help to establish a healthy pattern of prayer. I also feel like it will take some of the intimidation factor out of prayer for new believers. "How do we pray?"

Here are some suggestions. And I love how they are broken down daily and weekly and re-emphasize key points. I'm really excited to go through it again more slowly.

—Gina Davis

I am very impressed with the authenticity, heart, and vision that I have seen so far, and I am looking forward to diving into the rest of it.

Many books on prayer that I've started just don't resonate with me at all. This one does. Over the weekend I was eagerly telling my wife about it. Seriously…my life has been a bit crazy lately (which is another reason I need this book) but I am looking forward to continuing it!

—David Bouchard

I've been swamped lately. But the amazing, calming effect in just reading the intro and first three days is…is…healing.

—Eric Barron
CEO, the Steadfast Group

Table of Contents

PART ONE: INTRODUCTION **9**
   The Purpose of This Book 3
   This Book Is... 4
   This Book Is Not... 5
   How to Use This Book 7

PART TWO: PRINCIPLES **11**
   Pray with Regularity 13
   Pray with Your Bible 14
   Pray with Your Notes 14
   Pray with Your Pen 15
   Pray with Balance 16

PART THREE: PREPARATION **19**
   Set Apart This Time for God 21
   Sharpen Your Focus 24
      Focus on the Majesty of God 24
      Focus on the Love of God 24
      Focus on Your Relationship with God 25

PART FOUR: PRAYERS ... 27

Week 1: The Majestic God ... 29
- Day 1: God Is Present Everywhere ... 31
- Day 2: God Is Sovereign (1) ... 35
- Day 3: God Is Sovereign (2) ... 39
- Day 4: God Is Sovereign (3) ... 43
- Day 5: God Is Eternal (1) ... 47
- Day 6: God Is Eternal (2) ... 51
- Day 7: God Is All-Powerful ... 55

Week 2: The Gentle God ... 59
- Day 8: God Is Good (1) ... 61
- Day 9: God Is Good (2) ... 65
- Day 10: God Is Wise ... 69
- Day 11: God Is Patient (1) ... 73
- Day 12: God Is Patient (2) ... 77
- Day 13: God Is Love (1) ... 81
- Day 14: God Is Love (2) ... 85

Week 3: The Righteous God ... 89
- Day 15: God Is Holy (1) ... 91
- Day 16: God Is Holy (2) ... 95
- Day 17: God Is Our Rock ... 99
- Day 18: God Is Constant (Unchanging) ... 103
- Day 19: God Is Light ... 107
- Day 20: God Is a Righteous Judge (1) ... 111
- Day 21: God Is a Righteous Judge (2) ... 115

Week 4: The Merciful God ... 119
- Day 22: God Is Faithful (1) ... 121
- Day 23: God Is Faithful (2) ... 125
- Day 24: God Is Our Deliverer ... 129
- Day 25: God Is Merciful (1) ... 133
- Day 26: God Is Merciful (2) ... 137
- Day 27: God Is Near ... 141
- Day 28: God Is Our Salvation ... 145

Conclusion 149
    Celebrate Your Accomplishment 149
    What's Next? 150
    Additional Resources 150

APPENDIX A: BONUS DAYS 153
    Day 29: God Is Present Everywhere (2) 155
    Day 30: God Is All-Powerful (3) 159
    Day 31: God Is Faithful (3) 163

APPENDIX B: SCRIPTURE PRAYERS BY CATEGORY 167
    Adoration 169
    Confession 175
    Thanksgiving 183
    Supplication 191

REFERENCES 199
    Endnotes 199
    Cover Photo 199
    Scripture Translations Used 199

ACKNOWLEDGEMENTS 201

ABOUT THE AUTHOR 203
    Kevin T. Cunningham 203
    Websites 204
    Faith Story 205

PART ONE: INTRODUCTION

This book is written for people who long to love God with their whole being, but just need a little help.

Most people find spending time in prayer particularly challenging. They carve out some time. They muster up all their self-discipline and courage, get on their knees, and then say, "OK, what do I do now?!"

Personally, I have often found it helpful to have a variety of resources available to help me stay focused during prayer. I share this not because I am a spiritual giant. Rather, I often find it such a struggle to stay focused in prayer that I have had to discover or develop tools to help.

I have found three resources, or methods, immensely helpful in developing confidence and consistency in my own prayer life. In this book, we weave all three of those methods together for a powerful combination.

The Purpose of This Book

This book is designed to serve as a resource to help us grow closer to God and to build confidence and consistency in our personal prayer lives. Primarily, we need to remember that prayer is simply spending time with God. Unfortunately, we can complicate it so much that we get confused, insecure, bored, and distracted.

As we focus on God and spend time with him, we can bring our joys and needs to him. Then, we will be better able to partner with God in what he is looking to do in and through us.

At the heart of this book is a desire to help develop the habit of communicating with God in practical and powerful ways. Practical, because we will balance four different aspects of prayer. Powerful, because we will use God's Word as the basis for many of our prayers.

This book is filled with Scripture verses translated from the original languages that have been reworded into prayers. They are chosen to help us nurture and develop our focus on God and our love for him. As you get more comfortable with the concept, it will revolutionize the way you read your Bible.

This Book Is...

Very simply, this book is a prayer book. It is designed to help us pray, that is, to help us spend time with God. My goal is to help develop confidence and consistency in our personal prayer lives.

You may be able to read the book in one sitting, but that would miss the point. The book is organized so that you can choose one theme, centered on an attribute of God, each day. You can pray the paraphrased Scripture prayer in each section and follow it with your own personal prayers. Then, you may find yourself thinking about that attribute of God as you go through your day.

My focus is to help us get to know God a little better and to help us enjoy spending time with God. Therefore, I felt it important to occasionally use Yahweh in verses where the original Hebrew had YHWH for the name of God. In modern English translations, the names of God are usually rendered by certain fonts or variants of the word Lord since the exact pronunciation of the original is uncertain. Personally, I believe this leads to confusion for some people since *lord* can be such a generic term. It can be used to show general respect for any person or deity in control or with authority. This can lead to the "Aren't all gods really just the same with different names?" confusion. I thought it might be helpful to, at least occasionally, remind ourselves that we are praying to the Great I Am who is eternal, with neither beginning nor end and not dependent on anyone or anything else for his existence.

This Book Is Not...

Allow me to clarify potential misconceptions that might limit the effectiveness of this book in your life.

- This is not a book *about* prayer.

This book is designed to help us pray. It is not written to satisfy intellectual or theological curiosity about prayer. It is written to help us actually spend time with God.

Some of the concepts in this book may be new to you. I have tried to introduce these concepts in a way that will make them easy to understand and put into practice. I hope they prove helpful in your prayer life. But please know that they are only helpful if they lead to more, or more meaningful, time with God. Please don't allow yourself to quickly read through the content and put it back on the "shelf" without taking the time to implement the concepts, or thoughts they inspire, in your own time with God.

- This is not intended to replace your Bible.

This book is designed to supplement your personal Bible reading and to inspire us to remember that as we are reading God's Word, God is present with us.

I long to see this book inspire in us a habit of reading the Bible as a conversation with God. We can rejoice with the psalmists offering high praises to our God. We can repent with others when they are confronted with their sin, causing us to ask the Holy Spirit to reveal sin in our own lives. We can thank God for the way he acted in a particular passage. We can pray along with the authors of Scripture as they pray specifically for others or for general blessings and guidance.

- This is not a devotional book.

Typically, a devotional book will have a verse or brief passage of Scripture followed by inspirational writing to help appreciate or apply the biblical text. Devotional books can be of tremendous value, but this book is more of a workbook than a devotional. This book is designed to help us pray. We are encouraged to pray along with paraphrased Bible verses, but then we will also be encouraged to write or otherwise develop our own personalized prayers—based on other Scriptures, or your own thoughts and experiences.

- This book is not intended to settle theological disputes.

Even though the Scriptures are at the core of most of this book, when I translated these verses, my goal was to help us pray rather than preserve word for word accuracy.

Introduction

The prayers in this book are modifications or paraphrases of the original inspired verses. I have tried to honor the original intent of the verses but have reworded the verses to help us develop direct connection and communication with God.

Theology is the study of God. Prayer is time with God. This book is designed to help us grow closer to God through learning more about God and spending time with him. The book is organized around some of the attributes or characteristics of God. My hope is to reinforce and further stimulate our understanding of and devotion to God.

How to Use This Book

In the section titled Preparation, there are seven suggested prayers—one for each day of the week. May I suggest that you use any one of these prayers or something of your own creation to start your prayer time? It is just one way to remind ourselves that this time is set apart from the rest of our day.

Although we know God is present with us throughout our day, this time is specific in our focus and conversation with God. An analogy would be a married couple who may spend most of their Saturday in the same house, but at family dinnertime conversation is more direct and focused on each other. The TVs and Internet are turned off, and cell phones are put away because this is "time for us."

The main section of the book contains sets of daily prayers, each focusing on a different attribute of God. For each day, you will find:

- A very brief statement about the attribute or characteristic of God for the day.
- Four sections offering a suggested Scripture Prayer
- Four sections offering space for your own Personal Prayers.

Each day will include four groups of prayers, as mentioned earlier, organized by the acronym of ACTS, standing for Adoration, Confession, Thanksgiving, and Supplication.

Please pray the Scripture Prayer from each of the ACTS sections to God. If you feel led, you can use the spaces for Personal Prayers to write your own prayers in each category. Please don't feel compelled to write anything. Remember the focus is to grow closer to God by spending time with him meditating on who he is. There is no reason to feel that you need to fill in every blank line. You may feel more comfortable praying your own personal prayers without writing them down. That is totally fine!

Lastly, when praying in the Supplication (earnestly bringing our requests to God) sections, please note that many of the verses are focused on the needs of the person praying. As you feel led, please pray for other people by substituting their names for words like "me," "we," or "us." For example, in the Supplication section of the "God Is Love" chapter, we find this prayer:

> Lord, since you loved us in this way, surely we should love one another. Please help me to pass on the love that I have received.
> —Modified from 1 John 4:11

Introduction

After praying that God helps you pass on the love you have received from God, you could then pray the same prayer for any of your family members, friends, or even your pastor. You could pray...

> Lord, since you loved us in this way, surely we should love one another. Please help _____ to pass on the love that (he/she) has received.
> —Modified from 1 John 4:11

This will become second nature after you do it the first few times.

PART TWO: PRINCIPLES

Since you are reading a book that promised to help you (and me) develop confidence and consistency in our personal prayer life, I am writing with the assumption that you are open to a few suggestions. I commend you wholeheartedly for your commitment to spiritual growth.

I would like to suggest some foundational principles that will help prepare us for the journey ahead.

Pray with Regularity

I know. I know what you're saying—and with good reason. "If I could pray with regularity, I wouldn't have bought your book!" Please stay with me for a minute. Sometimes, it's easy to feel like life is out of control. But, I'm beginning to learn that we can probably change a lot more about our life than we think.

To begin developing consistency, try to identify—or carve out—a regular time and a regular place for your time with God. I understand it might seem like a stretch. It won't be easy. But you can do it—or at least get much closer than you think. If no time or place comes to mind, pray about it. Ask God specifically to help create a time and a place for you to meet with him. You'll be amazed what he can do. Remember, he is God!

Pray with Your Bible

Reading the Bible, even a small passage or chapter at a time, on a regular basis, gives us a chance to hear from God. He brings divine perspective into our daily lives.

Going deeper, when we read the Bible, we can talk with God about the Scriptures that he inspired. We can turn Bible verses into actual prayers for ourselves and others. There are some books that have already done that for us. The authors have reworded Bible verses into Scripture prayers. These can be especially helpful during stressful seasons of life. When we are under stress, all relationships are challenged—including our relationship with God. I have often found praying Scripture prayers helps me get started and focused. Then, my own prayers flow freely.

Additionally, sometimes we pray way too mildly because we may not be sure that something is God's will. Since the Bible is God's Word, God can use passages to stretch our thinking and our faith. As we allow the Scriptures to influence our prayers, we can be increasingly confident that we are aligned with God's will.

Pray with Your Notes

One reason many people lack consistency in their prayer life is simple disorganization. We want to pray for people and ministries, but we forget. Having some system to organize your prayer concerns will be a tremendous help.

This doesn't need to seem like homework. Keep it simple. You might use the notes feature on your phone. You might want to carry a pocket-sized notebook with you to jot down notes when you hear a request for prayer.

Some people use a larger notebook. I know a few people who create a page for each person and paste a small picture for a vivid reminder of the person as they pray. They also create sections for each day of the week. They divide their prayer concerns into different categories and pray for them once a week. Monday is for missionaries. Tuesday is for their kids' teachers (we may need to pray for them more than once a week). Wednesday is for…

Please note. If you are as organizationally challenged as I am, you may want to start small. Otherwise, you'll spend eternity searching for the perfect system and never actually start praying.

Pray with Your Pen

Many people find it helpful to write out their prayers. The process of writing their prayers helps them maintain focus and leaves a record to help track answers to prayer.

I admit this might take a little time to get used to. Even in our digital age, there is still something special about putting a pen to paper. It engages our mind and two of the five senses. This doesn't have to be formal or with perfect spelling and grammar. Remember the motto of the preschool teacher: Sometimes, the process is more important than the product.

You can make this as simple or as deluxe as you'd like. Some use a fancy leather-bound journal. Some just use a three-ring or spiral-bound notebook.

I have also found it helpful to combine this method with the ACTS pattern, which I'll explain in the next section below. You can take a sheet of paper and draw three lines across, making four sections. Write a simple but personal prayer for each of the four sections.

Pray with Balance

It is so easy to get out of balance in one direction or another. I have often found a pattern of prayer has helped me stay focused and balanced in my prayer life. This pattern helps us give attention to four vital areas of our relationship with God.

There are many prayer methods, systems, and tools. The ACTS pattern has been a tremendous help for me. This pattern is also scalable in that if I have sixty seconds or sixty minutes, the following four categories can help me stay on track.

>**ADORATION:** Begin your prayer time praising God for who He is—not just for what He has done for us (that will come later). This helps us focus on God himself. (Psalms 19, 29, 146-150)

>**CONFESSION:** After a time of focusing on the goodness and character of God, we can't help but see ourselves a little differently. Ask God to reveal the areas of your life that need attention—including wrong things we've done or good things we failed to do. (Psalms 32, 51, 139)

>**THANKSGIVING:** Now is the time to thank God for what he has done and for the many blessings that we enjoy. Sometimes, this comes easily. Sometimes, we need to make ourselves intentionally focus on what God has already done. (Psalm 50:1; 92:1; 35:18; Philippians 4:6)

>**SUPPLICATION:** Now is the time to bring our requests to God. Supplication is not a word most of us use every day, but it's a good word to use in this context. It has the idea of urgency or earnestness

(seriousness). We bring to God those items that have troubled or burdened our hearts, and we bring those requests to God. (1 Peter 5:7, Philippians 4:6-7)

ACTS is the classic order of this prayer pattern. However, occasionally, a different order might be more appropriate. For example, you might be bursting with appreciation because you just received a great blessing. Or, you may be overwhelmed with concern about a recent temptation that got the best of you. In those times, there is no need to slavishly follow a formula of prayer. This system should serve you—not restrain you.

PART THREE: PREPARATION

In our hurried and margin-less existence, we can often find ourselves rushing from one appointment to another, shifting from one interrupted task to the next, and from one interrupted conversation to another. Then we try to squeeze God in there someplace. We speed read a chapter of the Bible. We rush into church late trying to find a seat and catch up with worship. Then we wonder why we didn't get anything out of the service. But only for a minute because we have to get Jimmy to soccer practice after church.

Sometimes, it might be helpful to take a minute or two to get prepared and remind ourselves that we are meeting with the God of the universe. He is unequaled—in a class of his own. Like the couple in the previous chapter, we should make sure the TVs and Internet are turned off, and cell phones are, at least, on silent because this is time for us. Whether it is sixty minutes or just sixty seconds, this time is special.

Set Apart This Time for God

Let's make it clear to the spirit world and ourselves that we dedicate ourselves—and especially this time—to God.

The following prayers of dedication may be helpful. There is one entry for each day of the week. You could use these prayers to start your time with God each day. You may identify a prayer that particularly resonates with you and use that one more frequently. You may have other personal favorites that you might use instead of these. As with the rest of this book, please use this section in whatever way helps you draw closer to God.

- Monday

I love you, O Lord, my strength. I will call upon you Lord because you are worthy to be praised.

—Modified from Psalm 18:1, 3

- Tuesday

Dear Heavenly Father, thank you for this time that we can spend together. I am so grateful for your unfailing love, for I have put my trust in you. Show me the way I should walk, for I lift up my soul to you.

—Modified from Psalm 143:8-10

- Wednesday

Lord, in response to your mercies, I offer myself to you again this day as a living sacrifice, set apart for you. By faith in your Word, I know that my sacrifice will be acceptable to you. Please guide me during this time of prayer and throughout this day.

—Modified from Romans 12:1

- Thursday

I choose to give myself to you, my God, as one who has been made alive again, and I surrender my whole being to you to be used for your good purposes

—Modified from Romans 6:13, 19

- Friday

Lord, I agree with the heart of Joshua, "As for me and my house, we will serve the Lord." I commit myself to you again this day, asking for your blessing and protection on this house and this time that I can spend with you.

—Modified from Joshua 24:15

- Saturday

Lord, you are my God. I will exalt you! I will praise your name for you have done wonderful things, things planned long ago, in complete faithfulness and truth.

—Modified from Isaiah 25:1

- Sunday

I will sing praises to the Lord. I am one of your saints, and I will praise and give thanks to your holy name.

Modified from Psalm 30:4

Sharpen Your Focus.

Consider balancing these three suggestions to help direct your focus.

Focus on
the Majesty of God

We can come to God as beloved children. Sometimes, I need to remind myself that even though he invites us to call him Father, he is also still Almighty God. We are planning to spend some time with the God of the universe, so it can be helpful to be still for a few minutes (or at least a few seconds) to prepare our hearts and minds. Briefly meditating on Deuteronomy 4:39 has often helped me reorient my focus.

Acknowledge and take to heart this day that the LORD is God in heaven above and on the earth below. There is no other. (Deuteronomy 4:39 NIV)

He's the same God who told Moses, "Take your sandals off of your feet, for the place you are standing on is holy ground." (Genesis 3:5 WEB)

Focus on
the Love of God

God longs for us to spend quality time with him, more than we could possibly imagine. The Apostle John helps us put God's love into perspective. "For God so loved the world, that he gave his one and only Son, that whoever believes in him should not perish, but have eternal life." (John 3:16 WEB) "Consider the kind of extravagant love the Father has lavished on us—He calls us children of God! It's true; we are His beloved children." (1 John 3:1 VOICE)

God invites us to come to him with all of our joys, sorrows, and struggles. He even urges us to "come boldly to the throne of grace, that we may obtain mercy and find grace to help in time of need." (Hebrews 4:16 NKJV).

Focus on Your Relationship with God

Let's also remind ourselves that we are not here to check off an activity on our to-do list. We are here to spend time with God. Not time to learn about God. Time WITH God. He is here with you right now.

Jesus says, "I am standing at the door and knocking. If any of you hear my voice and open the door, then I will come in to visit with you and to share a meal at your table, and you will be with me." (Revelation 3:20 VOICE)

I have been marveling at how many kings and leaders in the Old Testament started out well for God only to drift from God into idolatry or sin by the end of their lives. All throughout time, we see the fickleness of humanity in hot, cold, and lukewarm responses to God's love. Through the prophet Isaiah, God said, "These people come near to me with their mouth and honor me with their lips, but their hearts are far from me." (Isaiah 29:13 NIV)

Jesus quoted that same passage when the Pharisees and teachers of the law asked him why his disciples didn't keep their traditions (Mark 7:5-7). Elsewhere in the New Testament, Jude urges his readers to "keep yourself in God's love" (Jude 1:21 WEB). The Apostle John records Jesus' strong rebuke to the church at Ephesus that even though they were very active, "you have left your first love" (Revelation 2:4 WEB). The NLT translates it as "You don't love me or each other as you did at first!"

There is a classic skit that vividly demonstrates how easy it is to forget that God is actually present when praying--TO HIM! [1]

Pray-er: "Our Father which art in heaven."

God: Yes?

Pray-er: Don't interrupt me. I'm praying.

God: But you called me.

Pray-er: Called you? I didn't call you. I'm praying. "Our Father which art in heaven.""

God: There, you did it again.

Pray-er: Did what?

God: Called me. You said, "Our Father which art in heaven." Here I am. What's on your mind?

Pray-er: But I didn't mean anything by it. I was, you know, just saying my prayers for the day. I always say the Lord's Prayer. It makes me feel good...

God: All right. Go on...

Now that we're prepared, let's spend some time with God.

PART FOUR: PRAYERS

Week 1:
The Majestic God

Week 1: The Majestic God

Day 1:
God Is Present Everywhere

God is spirit. He is not limited by space and time.

Scripture Prayers

Adoration

Lord, Heaven is your throne, and the earth is your footstool. Your hands have made both heaven and earth; they and everything in them are yours.
—Modified from Isaiah 66:1-2

Confession

Lord, please forgive me for thinking that I can hide from your presence when I want to indulge in bad choices or bad behavior. Please forgive me for forgetting that there is no place that is hidden from your sight.
—Inspired by Genesis 3:8-10

Day 1: God Is Present Everywhere

Thanksgiving

Lord, I am so grateful that you, O Lord, are high above all nations, your glory above the heavens. Who is like you, our God, who has his seat on high, and yet you stoop down to see in heaven and in the earth?

—Modified from Psalm 113:4-6

Supplication

(Pray this for yourself first. Then, pray it for someone else also.)

Lord, I know you commanded us to "Go, and make disciples of all nations, baptizing them and teaching them..." But, Lord, my favorite part is that you also reminded us that you are with us always, even to the end of the age. Lord, please help us to be faithful in partnering with you in sharing the gospel. Amen!

—Modified from Matthew 28:18-20

Personal Prayer

Adoration

Lord, I praise you because you are...

Confession

Lord, please forgive me for...

Thanksgiving

Lord, I thank you for...

Supplication

Lord, please...

Day 2:
God Is Sovereign (1)

God, alone, is the Lord over all creation.

Scripture Prayers

Adoration

Yours, O Lord, is the greatness and the power and the glory and the victory and the majesty, for all that is in the heavens and on the earth is yours. Yours is the kingdom, O Lord, and you are exalted as head above all. Both riches and honor come from you, and you reign over all. In your hand are power and might, and in your hand it is to make great and to give strength to all.
—Modified from 1 Chronicles 29:11-12

Confession

Lord, your Word clearly says that you are God in heaven above and on earth below. There is no other. Please forgive me for trying to rule my world instead of letting you have free reign in all of my life and my family.
—Modified from Deuteronomy 4:39

Thanksgiving

Lord, I am grateful that you are in charge. For you, my Lord, are God of gods and Lord of lords, the great, mighty, and awesome God, who is not partial and takes no bribe. You execute justice for the fatherless and the widow and love the sojourner, giving him food and clothing.
—Modified from Deuteronomy 10:17-18

Supplication

(Pray this for yourself first. Then, pray it for someone else also.)

Lord, by your Holy Spirit, please help us worship and bow down: Let us kneel before you, Lord, our maker. For you are our God, and we are the people of your pasture and the sheep of your hand. Lord, today if we hear your voice, please give us willing and obedient hearts to serve you with all our heart.
—Modified from Psalm 95:6-7

Personal Prayer

Adoration

Lord, I praise you because you are…

Confession

Lord, please forgive me for…

Thanksgiving

Lord, I thank you for…

Supplication

Lord, please…

Day 3:
God Is Sovereign (2)

God, alone, is the Lord over all creation.

Scripture Prayers

Adoration

There is no one like you, Yahweh; you are great and mighty. Who would not fear you, O King of the nations? For it belongs to you; because among all the wise men of the nations, and in all their royal estate, there is no one like you.
—Modified from Jeremiah 10:6-7

Confession

Lord, please forgive us for rejecting you. Forgive us for wanting to do things our own way. Just like Paul said of the lost, for although they knew you, they neither glorified you as God nor gave thanks to you, but their thinking became futile and their foolish hearts were darkened. Although they claimed to be wise, they became fools. We may not worship animals and statues, but if we are not careful, we can allow other things and people to take the place that you deserve in our lives.
—Modified from Romans 1:21-23

Day 3: God Is Sovereign (2)

Thanksgiving

Lord, I thank you that as the angel told Mary, I know that with you, nothing will be impossible.
—Modified from Luke 1:37

Supplication

(Pray this for yourself first. Then, pray it for someone else also.)

Lord, by your grace and through the work of your Holy Spirit, may I truly know and take this to heart this day. You, LORD, are God in heaven above and on the earth below. There is no other. May you truly be the Lord of my life today.
—Modified from Deuteronomy 4:39

Personal Prayer

Adoration

Lord, I praise you because you are…

Confession

Lord, please forgive me for…

Thanksgiving

Lord, I thank you for…

Supplication

Lord, please…

Day 4:
God Is Sovereign (3)

God, alone, is the Lord over all creation.

Scripture Prayers

Adoration

> You are great, O Lord God. For there is none like you, and there is no God besides you.
> —Modified from 2 Samuel 7:22

> O Lord, my Lord, how majestic is your name in all the earth!
> —Modified from Psalm 8:9

Confession

> Lord, please forgive us for times that we have hardened our hearts just like the Israelites did in the bitter uprisings in the wilderness. They tested you even though they had seen that nothing was too hard for you. Please forgive us for falling into the same temptation to grumble, complain, or rebel against you.
> —Modified from Psalm 95:8-9

Thanksgiving

O come, let us sing to the Lord: Let us make a joyful noise to the rock of our salvation. May we come before your presence with thanksgiving, and make a joyful noise to you with songs. For you, Lord, are a great God, and a great King above all gods.

—Modified from Psalm 95:1-3

Supplication

(Pray this for yourself first. Then, pray it for someone else also.)

Lord, may I like Rahab of Jericho recognize and proclaim that you are God in the heavens above and on the earth beneath.

—Modified from Joshua 2:11

Personal Prayer

Adoration

Lord, I praise you because you are...

Confession

Lord, please forgive me for...

Thanksgiving

Lord, I thank you for...

Supplication

Lord, please...

Day 5:
God Is Eternal (1)

God had no beginning and will live forever.

Scripture Prayers

Adoration

Now to the King eternal, immortal, invisible, to God, who alone is wise, be honor and glory forever and ever. Amen.

—Modified from 1 Timothy 1:17

Confession

O Lord (Yahweh), you are good and upright. You instruct sinners in the way they should go. You guide the humble in justice and teach the humble your way. All your paths are lovingkindness and truth to those who keep your covenant and testimonies. For your name's sake, O Lord, pardon my iniquity, for it is great. Please teach and guide me in your ways.

—Modified from Psalm 25:8-11

Day 5: God Is Eternal (1)

Thanksgiving

I am so grateful that you, Lord, reign! You are clothed with majesty and armed with strength. You established the world. It cannot be moved. Your throne is established from long ago. You are from everlasting. Your statutes stand firm. Holiness adorns your house, Yahweh, forevermore.

—Modified from Psalm 93:1-2

Supplication

(Pray this for yourself first. Then, pray it for someone else also.)

Lord, you are God, and there is no other. I know that you are God, and there is none like you. You declare the end from the beginning, and from ancient times things that are not yet done. Please guide us in your ways.

—Modified from Isaiah 46:9-10

Personal Prayer

Adoration

Lord, I praise you because you are...

Confession

Lord, please forgive me for...

Thanksgiving

Lord, I thank you for...

Supplication

Lord, please...

Day 6:
God Is Eternal (2)

God had no beginning and will live forever.

Scripture Prayers

Adoration

Lord, you have been our dwelling place for all generations. Before the mountains were born, before you had formed the earth and the world, even from everlasting to everlasting, you are God.
—Modified from Psalm 90:1-2

Confession

Lord, my sins are many and serious. But I take great comfort in your Word. For even though you live forever and your very name is holy, you also dwell with those who are brokenhearted over their own sin. Lord, please revive my spirit so that I don't lose heart because of my sin.
—Modified from Isaiah 57:15-16

Thanksgiving

Lord, I am so grateful that, since you are eternal, you can declare the end from the beginning and from ancient times things that are still to come.
—Modified from Isaiah 46:10

Supplication

(Pray this for yourself first. Then, pray it for someone else also.)

Lord, you see the end from the beginning. Please give me your perspective. I lift up my soul to you, O Lord. O my God, in you I trust. Show me your ways, O LORD, teach me your paths; guide me in your truth and teach me, for you are God my Savior. Please help me to trust in you all day long.
—Modified from Psalm 25:1-5

Personal Prayer

Adoration

Lord, I praise you because you are…

Confession

Lord, please forgive me for…

Thanksgiving

Lord, I thank you for…

Supplication

Lord, please…

Day 7:
God Is All-Powerful

There are no limits to God's power.

Scripture Prayers

Adoration

Now to you who are able to do so much more than all that we ask or think, according to the power that works in us. To you be the glory in the church and in Christ Jesus to all generations forever and ever. Amen.

—Modified from Ephesians 3:20-21

Confession

You are awesome, O God, in your holy place. You, Lord, give strength and power to your people. Praise be to God! Lord, please forgive me for relying on my own strength and forgetting that you long to grant us strength and power. Help me draw on your strength today.

—Modified from Psalm 68:35

Thanksgiving

Lord, I thank you that although there are many things that are impossible for mankind, we can rejoice that with you all things are possible.
—Modified from Matthew 19:26

Supplication

(Pray this for yourself first. Then, pray it for someone else also.)

I pray that the eyes of our hearts may be enlightened so that we may know the hope to which you have called us and what are the riches of the glory of your inheritance in your holy people and the exceeding greatness of your power toward us who believe.
—Modified from Ephesians 1:18-21

Personal Prayer

Adoration

Lord, I praise you because you are...

Confession

Lord, please forgive me for...

Thanksgiving

Lord, I thank you for...

Supplication

Lord, please...

Week 2:
The Gentle God

Day 8:
God Is Good (1)

God is pure and perfect in all he is and all he does.

Scripture Prayers

Adoration

I praise you, Lord, and I give thanks to you, Yahweh, for you are good, and your loving-kindness endures forever.
—Psalm 106:1

Confession

Lord, please forgive me for judging other people because of their sins as if my sins aren't that bad. Please forgive me for taking your goodness and patience for granted and forgetting that they are designed to lead me to repentance—not smugness! Please soften my heart that I might see my own sin from your perspective and turn back to you.
—Inspired by Romans 2:3-4

Thanksgiving

Thank you, Lord. I have tasted and seen that You, Yahweh, are indeed good. I am truly blessed because I take refuge in you.

—Modified from Psalm 34:8

Supplication

(Pray this for yourself first. Then, pray it for someone else also.)

Lord, please help me to wait patiently for you. Help me to be strong and courageous and wait patiently for you.

—Modified from Psalm 27:11-14

Personal Prayer

Adoration

Lord, I praise you because you are...

Confession

Lord, please forgive me for...

Thanksgiving

Lord, I thank you for...

Supplication

Lord, please...

Day 9:
God Is Good (2)

God is pure and perfect in all he is and all he does.

Scripture Prayers

Adoration

You, Lord, are good, and ready to forgive. You are abundant in loving-kindness to all those who call on you.

—Modified from Psalm 65:4

Confession

Lord, please forgive us for our many sins. Just like your children of old, we have sinned greatly even though you showered your goodness on us. Help us to live for you. Help our leaders to know and honor you.

—Modified from Nehemiah 9:32-35

Day 9: God Is Good (2)

Thanksgiving

Lord I give thanks to you, for you are good, for your loving-kindness endures forever.

—Modified from Psalm 118:1

Supplication

(Pray this for yourself first. Then, pray it for someone else also.)

Lord, I believe in your commandments. Please teach me good judgment and knowledge. You are good, and all you do is good. Teach me your statutes.

—Modified from Psalm 119:66-68

Personal Prayer

Adoration

Lord, I praise you because you are...

Confession

Lord, please forgive me for...

Thanksgiving

Lord, I thank you for...

Supplication

Lord, please...

Day 10:
God Is Wise

God exemplifies the ability to always make the best choices, flowing from his knowledge, character, and eternal perspective.

Scripture Prayers

Adoration

Lord, I praise you this day. Oh the depth of the riches both of your wisdom and your knowledge, O God! How unsearchable are your judgments, and your ways past tracing out!
—Modified from Romans 11:33

Confession

Lord, forgive me for allowing jealousy and selfish ambition anywhere near my heart. Help me remember that this "wisdom" is not from you, but is earthly, sensual, and demonic. For where jealousy and selfish ambition are, there is confusion and every evil deed.
—Modified from James 3:14-16

Day 10: God Is Wise

Thanksgiving

O, Lord, I thank you for your law. How I love it! It is my meditation all day. Your commandments make me wiser than my enemies, for your commandments are always with me. I have more understanding than all my teachers, for your testimonies are my meditation.

—Modified from Psalm 119:97-101

Supplication

(Pray this for yourself first. Then, pray it for someone else also.)

Lord, your Word tells us that "The fear of God is the beginning of knowledge, but the foolish despise wisdom and instruction." Lord, please help me to always give you the place of honor and respect you deserve in my life.

—Modified from Proverbs 1:7

Personal Prayer

Adoration

Lord, I praise you because you are...

Confession

Lord, please forgive me for...

Thanksgiving

Lord, I thank you for...

Supplication

Lord, please...

Day 11:
God Is Patient (1)

With eternity in mind, God is never rushed or frantic. He is not quickly angered and is often willing to allow people the time to process new thoughts.

Scripture Prayers

Adoration

> Lord, I do praise you today for you are indeed Yahweh, the Lord, the compassionate and gracious God, slow to anger, abounding in love and faithfulness.
> —Modified from Exodus 34:5-6

Confession

> Lord, please forgive us for, unlike you, we can be so quick to anger. Lord, help me remember that a gentle answer turns away wrath, but a harsh word stirs up anger.
> —Modified from Proverbs 15:1

Day 11: God Is Patient (1)

Thanksgiving

Lord, I thank you for your amazing patience as you waited for me to understand your gospel and repent from my own sins.

—Modified from 2 Peter 3:9

Supplication

(Pray this for yourself first. Then, pray it for someone else also.)

Lord, help me remember that a fool vents all of his anger, but a wise man brings himself under control. And that one who is slow to anger is better than the mighty; one who rules his own spirit is better than he who takes a city.

—Modified from Proverbs 16:32, 29:11

Personal Prayer

Adoration

Lord, I praise you because you are...

Confession

Lord, please forgive me for...

Thanksgiving

Lord, I thank you for...

Supplication

Lord, please...

Day 12:
God Is Patient (2)

With eternity in mind, God is never rushed or frantic. He is not quickly angered and is often willing to allow people the time to process new thoughts.

Scripture Prayers

Adoration

Lord, I praise you today because you are amazingly patient. Over and over again, your people, after trying your patience, declare that you are slow to anger and abounding in love.

—Modified from Psalm 103:8

Confession

Lord, please help us when we, like David, burn with anger against other people's sin. David said to Nathan, "As Yahweh lives, the man who has done this deserves to die!" But he was rebuked when Nathan replied, "You are that man." Help us realize that sometimes the sins that bother us the most are the very ones that we have also committed. Please help us acknowledge our own guilt and confess our sins.

—Modified from 2 Samuel 12:4-10

Thanksgiving

Lord, I thank you for the Holy Spirit, who is continually working in my life to develop patience in me (along with the other fruit of the Spirit).
—Modified from Galatians 5:22-25

Supplication

(Pray this for yourself first. Then, pray it for someone else also.)

Lord, help me remember that whoever is patient and slow to anger shows great understanding, but whoever has a quick temper highlights his foolishness.
—Modified from Proverbs 14:29

Personal Prayer

Adoration

Lord, I praise you because you are...

Confession

Lord, please forgive me for...

Thanksgiving

Lord, I thank you for...

Supplication

Lord, please...

Day 13:
God Is Love (1)

God proactively seeks the best for others even at great cost to himself.

Scripture Prayers

Adoration

> Your unfailing love is better than life itself; my lips will praise you! So, I will bless you while I live. I will lift up my hands in your name.
> —Modified from Psalm 63:3

Confession

> Please forgive me for not allowing your love to flow through me. So often, I am not patient or kind. Forgive me for times when I envy or brag, or am proud and seek my own way instead of what's better for others.
> —Modified from 1 Corinthians 13:4-5

Thanksgiving

Lord Jesus, I thank you that you demonstrated your own love for us in this: While we were still sinners, you died for us.

—Modified from Romans 5:8

Supplication

(Pray this for yourself first. Then, pray it for someone else also.)

Lord, please help us remember that you are our God and that you are the only God. Help us to love you as we should—with all our heart, with all our soul, with all our mind, and with all our strength. Also, please help us to love others as you would.

—Modified from Mark 12:29-30

Day 13: God Is Love (1)

Personal Prayer

Adoration

Lord, I praise you because you are...

Confession

Lord, please forgive me for...

Thanksgiving

Lord, I thank you for...

Supplication

Lord, please...

Day 14:
God Is Love (2)

God proactively seeks the best for others even at great cost to himself.

Scripture Prayers

Adoration

Lord, I am one of the redeemed, and I will proclaim it. I praise you, Yahweh, for your unfailing love and for your wonderful deeds to the children of men!

—Modified from Psalm 107:2, 8

Confession

Please forgive me, for often my life could not be summarized by "love." Please forgive me for not loving you or loving others the way I should.

—Inspired by 1 John 4:19

Thanksgiving

Lord, I thank you for how great a love you have given to us, that we should be called children of God!

—Modified from 1 John 3:1

Supplication

(Pray this for yourself first. Then, pray it for someone else also.)

Lord, remembering that we have the confidence to enter the Most Holy Place by the blood of Jesus, and that we have a great priest over the house of God, please help us draw near to you with a sincere heart and with the full assurance that faith brings. And Lord, the next time we attend any small group meeting or even a worship service, please show us how we can pass on your love to others by encouraging at least one person there.

—Modified from Hebrews 10:19-22

Day 14: God Is Love (2)

Personal Prayer

Adoration

Lord, I praise you because you are…

Confession

Lord, please forgive me for…

Thanksgiving

Lord, I thank you for…

Supplication

Lord, please…

Week 3:
The Perfect God

Day 15:
God Is Holy (1)

Holiness refers to something special—something that is set apart from the common things. God is completely different from his creation. He is in a class all his own—both in very nature and in moral purity.

Scripture Prayers

Adoration

Holy, holy, holy are you Lord God, Almighty, who was and who is and who is to come!
—Modified from Revelation 4:8

Confession

Lord, when I think of your holiness, I can't help but acknowledge that my sins are many and serious, but I take great comfort in your Word. You are the high and exalted one who is holy and who lives forever in a high and holy place. But you are also with the one who is contrite and humble in spirit, to revive the spirit of the humble and repentant. Lord, I do confess my sins, and I thank you for your forgiveness. Please help me live for you.
—Modified from Isaiah 57:15-16

Thanksgiving

Lord, I am grateful for your holiness. For there is no one as holy as you, Yahweh, for there is no one besides you, nor is there any rock like our God.
— Modified from 1 Samuel 2:2

Supplication

(Pray this for yourself first. Then, pray it for someone else also.)

Lord, please help me ascribe to you glory and strength...ascribe to you, O LORD, the glory due your name. May I worship you in the wonder of your holiness.
— Modified from Psalm 29:1-2

Personal Prayer

Adoration

Lord, I praise you because you are...

Confession

Lord, please forgive me for...

Thanksgiving

Lord, I thank you for...

Supplication

Lord, please...

Day 16:
God Is Holy (2)

Holiness refers to something special—something that is set apart from the common things. God is completely different from his creation. He is in a class all his own—both in very nature and in moral purity.

Scripture Prayers

Adoration

> Who is like you among the gods, O Lord? You are wonderful in power, awesome in glorious deeds, performing great wonders.
> —Modified from Exodus 15:11

Confession

> You commanded us to be holy to you; for you are holy, and you have set us apart from the peoples, that we should be yours. Lord, please forgive us for so easily getting distracted from our most important relationship—the one with you. Forgive us for being more concerned about pleasing other people than pleasing you.
> —Modified from Leviticus 20:26

Day 16: God Is Holy (2)

Thanksgiving

Lord, we rejoice with thankfulness, for you, the mighty one, have done great things for us. Holy is your name.

—Modified from Luke 1:49

Supplication

(Pray this for yourself first. Then, pray it for someone else also.)

Lord, our culture is so obsessed with sex; please give us your perspective. Please help us remember that your will for us is that we set ourselves apart and live holy lives. Lord, teach us how to take charge of our own bodies, maintaining purity and honor. May we not give in to the passion of lust or take advantage of anyone this way.

—Modified from 1 Thessalonians 4:3-8

Personal Prayer

Adoration

Lord, I praise you because you are...

Confession

Lord, please forgive me for...

Thanksgiving

Lord, I thank you for...

Supplication

Lord, please...

Day 17: God Is Our Rock

God is powerful and dependable.

Scripture Prayers

Adoration

Like Moses did, I will proclaim your name, O Lord. I will ascribe greatness to you, my God! You are the Rock, your work is perfect, for all your ways are just: You are a faithful God who never does wrong, just and right are you.
—Modified from Deuteronomy 32:3-4

Confession

Lord, please forgive me for turning from you, the God who can save me. I confess I have forgotten the Rock who can hide me. Even though I work hard, I don't have anything to show for it because I have not trusted in you, but sought help from those who only pretend to have your strength and ability to help.
—Modified from Isaiah 17:10

Thanksgiving

Lord, I thank you that you alone are my rock and my salvation, my fortress. I will not be shaken.
—Modified from Psalm 62:6

Supplication

(Pray this for yourself first. Then, pray it for someone else also.)

Lord, please help me not to give in to fear, or to be afraid. Help me remember that you declared it to us long ago, and have shown it. Lord, we are your witnesses. Is there a God besides you? Indeed, there is not. I don't know any other Rock.
—Modified from Isaiah 44:8

Personal Prayer

Adoration

Lord, I praise you because you are...

Confession

Lord, please forgive me for...

Thanksgiving

Lord, I thank you for...

Supplication

Lord, please...

Day 18:
God Is Constant (Unchanging)

God is the same yesterday, today, and forever. Since God is eternal and perfect, there is no need to improve and no danger of diminishing.

Scripture Prayers
Adoration

Lord, I praise you, for in the beginning, you laid the foundation of the earth. The heavens are the work of your hands. They will perish, but you will endure. Yes, all of them will wear out like a garment. You will change them like a cloak, and they will be changed. But you are the same. Your years will have no end.

—Modified from Psalm 102:25-27

Confession

Lord, please guide me in your truth and teach me, for you are the God of my salvation, I wait for you all day long. O Lord, you are the eternal one. Please do not hold the sins of my youth against me. Remember me according to your loving-kindness for your goodness' sake.

—Modified from Psalm 25:5-7

Thanksgiving

Lord, my days are as brief as a long shadow as the sun goes down. It will soon vanish like withered grass. But I am thankful that you, Yahweh, are enthroned forever; your renown endures to all generations.
—Modified from Psalm 102:11-12

Supplication

(Pray this for yourself first. Then, pray it for someone else also.)

Lord God, you are our God forever and ever. Please be our guide as long as we live.
—Modified from Psalm 48:14

Personal Prayer

Adoration

Lord, I praise you because you are…

Confession

Lord, please forgive me for…

Thanksgiving

Lord, I thank you for…

Supplication

Lord, please…

Day 19:
God Is Light

The Bible uses the word light to speak of illumination and moral purity. God is the source of both.

Scripture Prayers

Adoration

> Lord, I look forward to the day when we will no longer need the sun to shine by day, nor the moon to give its light by night, for you Lord, our God, will be our everlasting light, and our God will be our glory. Our sun will never set; our moon will not go down. For you, Lord, will be our everlasting light. Our days of mourning will come to an end.
> —Modified from Isaiah 60:19-20

Confession

> Lord, please forgive us for just drifting through life so distracted with just getting by. Forgive us for not realizing that the hour has come for us to wake up. For salvation is nearer to us now than when we first believed. Help us to cast off the works of darkness and put on the armor of light. Let us walk

Day 19: God Is Light

properly as in the daytime, not in drunkenness and immorality, not in arguing and jealousy. May we put on the Lord Jesus Christ, and make no provision for the flesh, to gratify its desires.

—Modified from Romans 13:11-14

Thanksgiving

Heavenly Father, I thank you for you made us fit to be partakers of the inheritance of the saints in light; you delivered us out of the power of darkness, and translated us into the Kingdom of the Son you love, in whom we have our redemption, the forgiveness of our sins. Hallelujah!

—Modified from Colossians 1:12-14

Supplication

(Pray this for yourself first. Then, pray it for someone else also.)

Lord, please help me receive your words of wisdom and store up your commands within me. May your wisdom and understanding keep me and deliver me from the way of evil, from those who speak perverse things and forsake the paths of uprightness to walk in the ways of darkness, who rejoice to do evil and delight in the perverseness of evil. Lord, please allow your light to help me see through their schemes.

—Modified from Proverbs 2:1, 10-14

Personal Prayer

Adoration

Lord, I praise you because you are…

Confession

Lord, please forgive me for…

Thanksgiving

Lord, I thank you for…

Supplication

Lord, please…

Week 3: The Righteous God

Day 20:
God Is a Righteous Judge (1)

God is able to judge impartially and with eternal wisdom and perspective.

Scripture Prayers

Adoration

Lord, I praise you today for you are righteous. When you pronounced judgment from heaven, the earth feared and was silent. When you arose to judgment, you saved all the afflicted ones of the earth.
—Modified from Psalm 76:8-9

Confession

Lord, please forgive me for lacking humility and jumping at the chance to find fault in others, to complain about or even judge them. Please forgive me for forgetting that you alone are the righteous judge who is able to save and to destroy. Please forgive me for judging other people.
—Modified from James 4:10-12

Thanksgiving

Lord, I thank you for not abandoning us in your wrath, but rather you loved us so much that you gave your one and only Son, that whoever believes in him should not perish, but have eternal life. For you didn't send your Son into the world to judge the world, but that the world should be saved through him.

—Modified from John 3:16-17

Supplication

(Pray this for yourself first. Then, pray it for someone else also.)

Lord, I think of the Apostle Paul toward the end of his years on earth saying, "I have fought the good fight. I have finished the course. I have kept the faith" and knowing that he would receive a crown of righteousness from you, the Righteous Judge. Lord, please help me live my life today in such a way that I would look forward to the Day of Judgment when you appear.

—Modified from 2 Timothy 4:7-8

Day 20: God Is a Righteous Judge (1)

Personal Prayer

Adoration

Lord, I praise you because you are...

Confession

Lord, please forgive me for...

Thanksgiving

Lord, I thank you for...

Supplication

Lord, please...

Day 21:
God Is a Righteous Judge (2)

God is able to judge impartially and with eternal wisdom and perspective.

Scripture Prayers

Adoration

Lord, I praise you today just as Moses did after you delivered your people through the Red Sea. I will sing to you, LORD, for you have triumphed gloriously. You are my strength and my song, and you have rescued me. You are my God, and I will praise you.

—Modified from Exodus 15:1-2

Confession

Lord, please forgive us and heal our land. We've pushed you out of our schools and our public forums. We've exchanged the truth for a lie, and worshiped and served the creature rather than you, our Creator. You have allowed our culture to spiral downward to ever increasing levels of spiritual and moral corruption.

—Modified from Romans 1:28-32

Thanksgiving

Lord, I thank you for the new life you have given us. Even though we were dead in transgressions and sins, you, being rich in love and mercy, made us alive together with Christ. Lord, I know it is by grace we have been saved. Lord, not only did you make us alive with your Son, but you raised us up with him, and made us to sit with him in the heavenly places in Christ Jesus.

—Modified from Ephesians 2:1-6

Supplication

(Pray this for yourself first. Then, pray it for someone else also.)

Heavenly Father, you have told us that you love the Son and have given all things into his hand. I know that whoever believes in the Son has eternal life; whoever does not obey the Son shall not see life, but the wrath of God remains on him. Lord, please help me understand the seriousness and the urgency of introducing people to your Son. Please guide me and empower me by your Holy Spirit that I may know how to share the gospel with clarity, love, gentleness, respect, and boldness.

–Inspired by John 3:35-36; Colossians 4:4; Ephesians 6:20; 1 Peter 3:15

Day 21: God Is a Righteous Judge (2)

Personal Prayer

Adoration

Lord, I praise you because you are...

Confession

Lord, please forgive me for...

Thanksgiving

Lord, I thank you for...

Supplication

Lord, please...

Week 4:
The Merciful God

Day 22:
God Is Faithful (1)

God can and will do what he has promised.

Scripture Prayers

Adoration

I will sing of the mercies of the Lord forever: I will tell of your faithfulness to all generations.
—Modified from Psalm 89:1

Confession

Lord, I read in your Word that like so many other kings, Zedekiah did what was evil in your sight even though you were the Lord his God, and he refused to humble himself... Likewise, all the leaders of the priests and the people became more and more unfaithful. Lord, please forgive our leaders—both in the church and in the government—for being unfaithful to you. It is so easy to drift from worshiping and trusting you, to trusting in ourselves or looking for help from others. Lord, please forgive our sins.
—Modified from 2 Chronicles 36:12-14

Day 22: God Is Faithful (1)

Thanksgiving

Lord, I thank you that you are faithful and will not allow us to be tempted above what we are able, but with the temptation will also provide the way of escape, that we may be able to endure it. Lord, I also thank you that when we neglect to use the "way of escape" that you had provided and stumble into sin, that you still remain faithful. For you have promised if we confess our sins, you are faithful and righteous to forgive our sins, and to cleanse us from all unrighteousness.
—Modified from 1 Corinthians 10:13 and 1 John 1:9

Supplication

(Pray this for yourself first. Then, pray it for someone else also.)

Lord, may I be like Sarah, who even though she initially laughed at the thought of having a child in her old age, knew that you were faithful and would keep your promise. May I be able to trust your faithfulness to do what you have promised even though I may not understand how.
—Modified from Genesis 18:9-15 and Hebrews 11:11

Personal Prayer

Adoration

Lord, I praise you because you are...

Confession

Lord, please forgive me for...

Thanksgiving

Lord, I thank you for...

Supplication

Lord, please...

Day 23:
God Is Faithful (2)

God can and will do what he has promised.

Scripture Prayers

Adoration

Your unfailing love, O LORD, is as vast as the heavens; your faithfulness reaches beyond the clouds. Your righteousness is like the mighty mountains, your justice like the ocean depths.
—Modified from Psalm 36:5-6

Confession

Please forgive me for taking your faithfulness for granted. Please forgive me for my sin and help me to choose the way of escape that you provide rather than the momentary pleasure of sin.
—Modified from 1 Corinthians 10:13

Day 23: God Is Faithful (2)

Thanksgiving

Dear God, I rejoice in your faithfulness. I know that you are not a man, that you should lie, nor the son of man, that you should repent. Have you said something, and will you not do it? Or have you spoken, and will you not make it good?
—Modified from Numbers 23:19

Supplication

(Pray this for yourself first. Then, pray it for someone else also.)

Lord, help us to not be worried about the future. Help us to trust you knowing that you are faithful. Lord, as the God of peace, may you sanctify us completely. May our whole spirit, soul, and body be preserved blameless at the coming of your Son, our Lord Jesus Christ.
—Modified from 1 Thessalonians 5:23-24

Week 4: The Merciful God

Day 23: God Is Faithful (2)

Personal Prayer

Adoration

Lord, I praise you because you are...

Confession

Lord, please forgive me for...

Thanksgiving

Lord, I thank you for...

Supplication

Lord, please...

Day 24:
God Is Our Deliverer

Because God is sovereign, powerful, and merciful, he is willing and able to deliver us.

Scripture Prayers

Adoration

I love you, O LORD, my strength. You, LORD, are my rock, and my fortress, and my deliverer; My God, my strength, in whom I trust; My shield, and the horn of my salvation, and my high tower. I will call upon you, LORD, for you are worthy to be praised: So shall I be saved from my enemies.
—Modified from Psalm 18:1–3

Confession

Lord, I call out to you; you are my Rock, do not turn a deaf ear to me. For if you remain silent, it would be as if I were already dead. Hear my cry for mercy as I call to you for help, as I lift up my hands in prayer toward your Most Holy Place.
—Modified from Psalm 28:1-2

Thanksgiving

Lord, I proclaim that you alone are my rock. Lord, I thank you that by your grace, we, like living stones, are being built up as a spiritual house, to be a holy priesthood, to offer up spiritual sacrifices acceptable to you through Jesus Christ. By your grace, we are a chosen race, a royal priesthood, a holy nation, a people for your own possession, Lord, so that we may proclaim that you are the one who called us out of darkness into your marvelous light.

—Modified from 1 Peter 2:1-10

Supplication

(Pray this for yourself first. Then, pray it for someone else also.)

May the words of my mouth and the meditation of my heart be pleasing to you, O Lord, my rock, and my redeemer.

—Modified from Psalm 19:14

Personal Prayer

Adoration

Lord, I praise you because you are...

Confession

Lord, please forgive me for...

Thanksgiving

Lord, I thank you for...

Supplication

Lord, please...

Day 25:
God Is Merciful (1)

Because God is merciful, we are spared the punishment our sins deserve.

Scripture Prayers

Adoration

Lord, I praise you for you are full of compassion and mercy.
—Modified from James 5:11

Confession

Lord, my sin causes me to despair sometimes; please forgive me for my sin and for doubting your forgiveness. I know it is because of your amazing love that we are not consumed because your mercies never fail. Indeed, they are new every morning; great is your faithfulness.
—Modified from Lamentations 3:21-23

Thanksgiving

Lord, I am so grateful that even though we were once far from you, you showed us your mercy. We were foolish, disobedient, deceived, and enslaved by various desires and "pleasures," living in malice and envy—hating and being hated. But you saved us, not because of any "good works" that we had done, but because of your mercy, you saved us through the work of the Holy Spirit cleansing us and giving us new life.

—Modified from Titus 3:3-5

Supplication

(Pray this for yourself first. Then, pray it for someone else also.)

Lord, please help us to have right priorities. Lord, you have shown us what is good. What do you, Yahweh, require of us, but to act justly, to love mercy, and to walk humbly with our God. Realizing how mercy is such a part of who you are, please help me this day to love people by showing mercy to those you put in my path.

—Inspired by Micah 6:8

Personal Prayer

Adoration

Lord, I praise you because you are...

Confession

Lord, please forgive me for...

Thanksgiving

Lord, I thank you for...

Supplication

Lord, please...

Day 26:
God Is Merciful (2)

Because God is merciful, we are spared the punishment our sins deserve.

Scripture Prayers

Adoration

Lord, I praise you because you are rich in mercy.
—Modified from Ephesians 2:4

Confession

Lord Jesus, I thank you for being a great high priest, able to sympathize with our weaknesses. For you too were tempted in all things, just like us, but you faced those temptations without yielding to sin. Please forgive me for my sins and help me to live for you.
—Modified from Hebrews 4:14-15

Thanksgiving

Lord, I am so thankful that you are merciful, especially when I remember that I was spiritually dead in my own transgressions and sins. But, because you are so rich in mercy and you loved us so much, you made us alive, together with your Son, Jesus. That would have been more than enough. But you even raised us and seated us in heavenly places in Christ Jesus.
—Modified from Ephesians 2:4-6

Supplication

(Pray this for yourself first. Then, pray it for someone else also.)

Lord, we know that you are a God of mercy; please help us come boldly to your throne of grace, that we may receive mercy in our times of need.
—Modified from Hebrews 4:16

Personal Prayer

Adoration

Lord, I praise you because you are...

Confession

Lord, please forgive me for...

Thanksgiving

Lord, I thank you for...

Supplication

Lord, please...

Day 27:
God Is Near

God is spirit. He is not limited by the confines of space and time.

Scripture Prayers

Adoration

> Lord Jesus, I praise you. Although you were essentially one with God and in the form of God, you didn't hold on to your status and privileges. Instead, you took on the form of a servant and the likeness of a newborn baby human.
> —Modified from Philippians 2:6-7

Confession

> Lord, your Word says we are to be free from the love of money and be satisfied with what we have, for you have promised, "I will in no way leave you, and neither will I in any way forsake you."
> Please forgive me for not being content with your love, your presence, and your gifts in my life and for so easily getting distracted—pursuing other things that promise fulfillment.
> —Inspired by Hebrews 13:5

Thanksgiving

What great nation is there that has a god so near to it as is the LORD our God whenever we call on Him? Lord, I thank you that you are near and that you invite us to call on you.

—Modified from Deuteronomy 4:7

Supplication

(Pray this for yourself first. Then, pray it for someone else also.)

Lord, you have promised that when the righteous cry, you hear and deliver them out of all their anguish. You are near to those who are discouraged and have lost all hope. Please help me be aware of your presence and comfort in my life today.

—Modified from Psalm 34:17-18

Personal Prayer

Adoration

Lord, I praise you because you are...

Confession

Lord, please forgive me for...

Thanksgiving

Lord, I thank you for...

Supplication

Lord, please...

Day 28:
God Is Our Salvation

God is both the judge who pronounces the sentence and the savior; he takes our deserved punishment upon himself so that we may be free.

Scripture Prayers

Adoration

The Lord lives, and blessed be my rock, and let the God of my salvation be exalted.
—Modified from Psalm 18:46

Confession

Lord, please forgive me for trying to build my life on a foundation other than your commands and precepts. Lord, forgive me for being like the man who hears your words and doesn't do what you've said. It's like building a house without a foundation, against which the stream broke, and immediately it fell, and the ruin of that house was great. Please forgive me for making a mess of things. Please help me build my life on your truths. Only then will I be able to withstand the storms of life.
—Inspired by Luke 6:47-49

Day 28: God Is Our Salvation

Thanksgiving

Lord, I thank you that you hear my cry, dear God and that you listen to my prayer. From the end of the earth, I will call to you, when my heart is overwhelmed. Lead me to the rock that is higher than I. For you have been a refuge for me, a strong tower from the enemy. I will dwell in your tent forever. I will take refuge in the shelter of your wings.

—Modified from Psalm 61:1-4

Supplication

(Pray this for yourself first. Then, pray it for someone else also.)

Lord, please help us remember we don't belong in this world. Help us resist those desires of the flesh that battle against our soul. May we live lives of integrity among the people so that, even when some may be inclined to call us evildoers, they see our good works and might give glory to you when you return.

—Modified from 1 Peter 2:11-12

Day 28: God Is Our Salvation

Personal Prayer

Adoration

Lord, I praise you because you are...

Confession

Lord, please forgive me for ...

Thanksgiving

Lord, I thank you for...

Supplication

Lord, please ...

Conclusion

Congratulations! Before we focus on the next steps, I want you to savor the victory a little bit. You've made it through the past four weeks. I am proud of you and truly hope you have enjoyed the journey.

Celebrate Your Accomplishment

Over the past four weeks, you have learned, or reinforced, how easy and exciting it can be to pray through verses or themes in the Bible. If you have been using the Personal Prayer sections, you have also seen how praying paraphrased Scripture Prayers can prompt and inspire your own prayers.

You have also learned, or reinforced, a pattern of prayer that helps us balance four key aspects of prayer. You've developed a habit of thinking in terms of

- praising God for who he is (Adoration),
- admitting and confessing your sins (Confession),
- thanking God for what he has done (Thanksgiving), and
- bringing your requests to God for yourself and for others (Supplication).

You have spent the past four weeks focusing on four seemingly contradictory aspects of God's character. We have seen how all of God's attributes live in perfect harmony without confusion or contradiction. This fuller view of God will help us interpret our Bible study in new ways.

What's Next?

Allow the ACTS pattern of prayer to continue to guide your thoughts. You will find praying through the four categories will become a natural part of your day. Eventually, you will find yourself waiting in traffic or in line at the grocery store, and the Holy Spirit will bring this pattern to mind.

If this resource has helped you grow closer to God, please feel free to use the Bonus material in Appendix A, or start over again from Day 1. Appendix B has all the Scripture Prayers organized by the ACTS categories. You can highlight prayers that are particularly meaningful for future use.

Additional Resources

Personally, I have found that having some resources like this has been a great asset to help me stay focused and keep my personal time with God vibrant and fresh.

I have included some resources below that I have personally found very helpful in my prayer times. I can wholeheartedly recommend these if you are seeking additional resources to help you grow spiritually. Please visit www.EncourageAndEquip.com/twg for an updated list with clickable links that will help support future writing projects.

- Boa, Kenneth, *Handbook to Prayer: Praying Scripture Back to God*
  Available in Kindle ebook on Amazon.

- King, Tiece L., *Pray the Word: 90 Prayers That Touch the Heart of God*
  Available in paperback and Kindle ebook on Amazon.

  King, Tiece L., *Pray the Word for Your Church*
  Available in paperback and Kindle ebook on Amazon.

  King, Tiece L., *31 Days of Praying the Word*
  Free download available in English, Thai, Chinese, Spanish, Japanese, and Indonesian. Mobile app and additional prayer resources are also available for download.

- Moore, Beth, *Praying God's Word: Breaking Free from Spiritual Strongholds*
  Available in hardcover, paperback, Kindle ebook, Audible audiobook, and audio CD on Amazon.

- Spangler, Ann, *Praying the Names of God: A Daily Guide*
  Available in hardcover, paperback, Kindle ebook, and Audible audiobook on Amazon.

  Spangler, Ann, *Praying the Attributes of God: A Daily Guide to Experiencing His Greatness*
  Available in hardcover on Amazon.

- Whitney, Donald S., *Praying the Bible*
  Available in hardcover, Kindle ebook, Audible audiobook, and audio CD on Amazon.

APPENDIX A: BONUS DAYS

Day 29:
God Is Present Everywhere (2)

God is spirit. He is not limited by space and time.

Scripture Prayers

Adoration

> Lord God, along with the seraphim, I praise you today. Holy, holy, holy is the Lord of hosts: The whole earth is full of your glory.
> —Modified from Isaiah 6:3

Confession

> I confess that I can lose sight of your presence and work in my life and drift into sin. But I take great comfort, Lord, that even though you are the high and holy God, who lives forever, and you live in a high and holy place, I rejoice that you also live with people who are humble and repentant, so that you can restore our confidence and hope.
> —Modified from Isaiah 57:15

Thanksgiving

Lord, I thank you that you are not limited by any boundaries. I rejoice that you are a God close by and far off also—you fill heaven and earth!
—Modified from Jeremiah 23:23-24

Supplication

(Pray this for yourself first. Then, pray it for someone else also.)

Lord, you have promised that where two or three are gathered together in your name, you are present among them. Lord, when we meet for worship, with our small group or even with some friends for dinner, please help us be aware that you are right there with us.
—Modified from Matthew 18:20

Day 29: God Is Present Everywhere (2)

Personal Prayer

Adoration

Lord, I praise you because you are...

Confession

Lord, please forgive me for...

Thanksgiving

Lord, I thank you for...

Supplication

Lord, please...

Day 30:
God Is All-Powerful (3)

There are no limits to God's power.

Scripture Prayers

Adoration

Lord, I praise you because I know that you are the God of all peoples. You have made the heavens and the earth by your great power and by your outstretched arm. Nothing is too hard for you.
—Modified from Genesis 18:14, Jeremiah 32:27

Confession

Lord, I know that we didn't choose you, but you chose us, and appointed us, that we should go and bear fruit, and that our fruit should remain; that whatever we ask you, in the name of your son, Jesus, you already long to give to us. Please forgive me for getting so easily distracted by the cares of this life that I don't bear fruit for you and that I so often look to resolve my challenges in my own "strength" and forget that you, the Almighty God, long for me to bring my needs before you.
—Modified from John 15:16

Day 30: God Is All-Powerful (3)

Thanksgiving

You said to Jacob, "I am El-Shaddai—God Almighty. Be fruitful and multiply. You will become a great nation, even many nations. Kings will be among your descendants!" Lord, I thank you for fulfilling your promise. You are indeed almighty and faithful.

—Modified from Genesis 35:11

Supplication

(Pray this for yourself first. Then, pray it for someone else also.)

Lord, I want to praise you as I should. Please help me make a joyful shout to you! Help me sing to the glory of your name! Help me proclaim, "How awesome are your deeds! Through the greatness of your power, your enemies submit themselves to you. All the earth will worship you, and will sing to you; they will sing to your name."

—Modified from Psalm 66:1-4

Day 30: God Is All-Powerful (3)

Personal Prayer

Adoration

Lord, I praise you because you are...

Confession

Lord, please forgive me for...

Thanksgiving

Lord, I thank you for...

Supplication

Lord, please...

Day 31:
God Is Faithful (3)

God can and will do what he has promised.

Scripture Prayers

Adoration

Lord, your kingdom is an everlasting kingdom. Your dominion endures throughout all generations. You are eternal and faithful in all your words, and loving in all your deeds.
—Modified from Psalm 145:13

Confession

Lord, you often refer to your relationship with your people in terms of a marriage. You also warn us that the ways of this world are very different from your ways. Lord, please forgive us for being like an unfaithful spouse, being so easily distracted from the simplicity and purity of devotion to Christ.
—Inspired by Isaiah 62:5, John 17:14, 2 Corinthians 11:3

Thanksgiving

Lord, I am so thankful that your faithful love never ends! Your mercies never cease. It is by your mercies, O Lord, that we are not consumed, because your compassions fail not. They are new every morning: Great is your faithfulness.

—Modified from Lamentations 3:22-23

Supplication

(Pray this for yourself first. Then, pray it for someone else also.)

Lord, seeing how faithful you are by your very nature, please help me to be faithful to you and to those around me. Lord, please help me to be faithful in the very little, that you may be able to trust me with greater responsibilities.

—Inspired by Luke 16:10-12

Personal Prayer

Adoration

Lord, I praise you because you are…

Confession

Lord, please forgive me for…

Thanksgiving

Lord, I thank you for…

Supplication

Lord, please…

APPENDIX B: SCRIPTURE PRAYERS BY CATEGORY

Adoration

Lord, Heaven is your throne, and the earth is your footstool. Your hands have made both heaven and earth; they and everything in them are yours.
—Modified from Isaiah 66:1-2

Yours, O Lord, is the greatness and the power and the glory and the victory and the majesty, for all that is in the heavens and on the earth is yours. Yours is the kingdom, O Lord, and you are exalted as head above all. Both riches and honor come from you, and you reign over all. In your hand are power and might, and in your hand it is to make great and to give strength to all.
—Modified from 1 Chronicles 29:11-12

There is no one like you, Yahweh; you are great and mighty. Who would not fear you, O King of the nations? For it belongs to you; because among all the wise men of the nations, and in all their royal estate, there is no one like you.
—Modified from Jeremiah 10:6-7

You are great, O Lord God. For there is none like you, and there is no God besides you.
—Modified from 2 Samuel 7:22

O Lord, my Lord, how majestic is your name in all the earth!
—Modified from Psalm 8:9

Now to the King eternal, immortal, invisible, to God, who alone is wise, be honor and glory forever and ever. Amen.
—Modified from 1 Timothy 1:17

Lord, you have been our dwelling place for all generations. Before the mountains were born, before you had formed the earth and the world, even from everlasting to everlasting, you are God.
—Modified from Psalm 90:1-2

Now to you who are able to do so much more than all that we ask or think, according to the power that works in us. To you be the glory in the church and in Christ Jesus to all generations forever and ever. Amen.
—Modified from Ephesians 3:20-21

I praise you, Lord, and I give thanks to you, Yahweh, for you are good, and your loving-kindness endures forever.
—Modified from Psalm 106:1

You, Lord, are good, and ready to forgive. You are abundant in loving-kindness to all those who call on you.
—Modified from Psalm 65:4

Lord, I praise you this day. Oh the depth of the riches both of your wisdom and your knowledge, O God!

Adoration

How unsearchable are your judgments, and your ways past tracing out!
—Modified from Romans 11:33

Lord, I do praise you today for you are indeed Yahweh, the Lord, the compassionate and gracious God, slow to anger, abounding in love and faithfulness.
—Modified from Exodus 34:5-6

Lord, I praise you today because you are amazingly patient. Over and over again, your people, after trying your patience, declare that you are slow to anger and abounding in love.
—Modified from Psalm 103:8

Your unfailing love is better than life itself; my lips will praise you! So, I will bless you while I live. I will lift up my hands in your name.
—Modified from Psalm 63:3

Lord, I am one of the redeemed, and I will proclaim it. I praise you, Yahweh, for your unfailing love and for your wonderful deeds to the children of men!
—Modified from Psalm 107:2, 8

Holy, holy, holy are you Lord God, Almighty, who was and who is and who is to come!
—Modified from Revelation 4:8

Who is like you among the gods, O Lord? You are wonderful in power, awesome in glorious deeds, performing great wonders.
—Modified from Exodus 15:11

Like Moses did, I will proclaim your name, O Lord. I will ascribe greatness to you, my God! You are the Rock,

your work is perfect, for all your ways are just: You are a faithful God who never does wrong, just and right are you.
—Modified from Deuteronomy 32:3-4

Lord, I praise you, for in the beginning, you laid the foundation of the earth. The heavens are the work of your hands. They will perish, but you will endure. Yes, all of them will wear out like a garment. You will change them like a cloak, and they will be changed. But you are the same. Your years will have no end.
—Modified from Psalm 102:25-27

Lord, I look forward to the day when we will no longer need the sun to shine by day, nor the moon to give its light by night, for you Lord, our God, will be our everlasting light, and our God will be our glory. Our sun will never set; our moon will not go down. For you, Lord, will be our everlasting light. Our days of mourning will come to an end.
—Modified from Isaiah 60:19-20

Lord, I praise you today for you are righteous. When you pronounced judgment from heaven, the earth feared and was silent. When you arose to judgment, you saved all the afflicted ones of the earth.
—Modified from Psalm 76:8-9

Lord, I praise you today just like Moses did after you delivered your people through the Red Sea and from the hands of the Egyptian army.

I will sing to you, LORD, for you have triumphed gloriously, the horse and rider thrown into the sea. You are my strength and my song, and you have rescued me. You are my God, and I will praise you.
—Modified from Exodus 15:1-2

Adoration

I will sing of the mercies of the Lord forever: I will tell of your faithfulness to all generations.
—Modified from Psalm 89:1

Your unfailing love, O LORD, is as vast as the heavens; your faithfulness reaches beyond the clouds. Your righteousness is like the mighty mountains, your justice like the ocean depths.
—Modified from Psalm 36:5-6

I love you, O LORD, my strength. You, LORD, are my rock, and my fortress, and my deliverer; My God, my strength, in whom I trust; My shield, and the horn of my salvation, and my high tower. I will call upon you, LORD, for you are worthy to be praised: So shall I be saved from my enemies.
—Modified from Psalm 18:1–3

Lord, I praise you for you are full of compassion and mercy.
—Modified from James 5:11

Lord, I praise you because you are rich in mercy.
—Modified from Ephesians 2:4

Lord Jesus, I praise you. Although you were essentially one with God and in the form of God, you didn't hold on to your status and privileges. Instead, you took on the form of a servant and the likeness of a newborn baby human.
—Modified from Philippians 2:6-7

The Lord lives, and blessed be my rock, and let the God of my salvation be exalted.
—Modified from Psalm 18:46

Lord God, along with the seraphim, I praise you today. Holy, holy, holy is the Lord of hosts: The whole earth is full of your glory.

—Modified from Isaiah 6:3

Lord, I praise you because I know that you are the God of all peoples. You have made the heavens and the earth by your great power and by your outstretched arm. There is nothing too hard for you.

—Modified from Genesis 18:14, Jeremiah 32:27

Lord, your kingdom is an everlasting kingdom. Your dominion endures throughout all generations. You are eternal and faithful in all your words, and loving in all your deeds.

—Modified from Psalm 145:13

Confession

Lord, please forgive us for thinking that we can hide from your presence when we want to indulge in bad choices or bad behavior. Please forgive us for forgetting that there is no place that is hidden from your sight.
—Inspired by Genesis 3:8-10

Lord, your Word clearly says that you are God in heaven above and on earth below. There is no other. Please forgive me for trying to rule my world instead of letting you have free reign in all of my life and my family.
—Modified from Deuteronomy 4:39

Lord, please forgive us for rejecting you. Forgive us for wanting to do things our own way. Just like Paul said of the lost, for although they knew you, they neither glorified you as God nor gave thanks to you, but their thinking became futile and their foolish hearts were darkened. Although they claimed to be wise, they became fools. We may not worship animals and statues, but if we

are not careful, we can allow other things and people to take the place that you deserve in our lives.
—Modified from Romans 1:21-23

Lord, please forgive us for times that we have hardened our hearts just like the Israelites did in the bitter uprisings in the wilderness. They tested you even though they had seen that nothing was too hard for you. Please forgive us for falling into the same temptation to grumble, complain, or rebel against you.
—Modified from Psalm 95:8-9

O Lord (Yahweh), you are good and upright. You instruct sinners in the way they should go. You guide the humble in justice and teach the humble your way. All your paths are lovingkindness and truth to those who keep your covenant and testimonies. For your name's sake, O Lord, pardon my iniquity, for it is great. Please teach and guide me in your ways.
—Modified from Psalm 25:8-11

Lord, my sins are many and serious. But I take great comfort in your Word. For even though you live forever and your very name is holy, you also dwell with those who are brokenhearted over their own sin. Lord, please revive my spirit so that I don't lose heart because of my sin.
—Modified from Isaiah 57:15-16

You are awesome, O God, in your holy place. You, Lord, give strength and power to your people. Praise be to God! Lord, please forgive me for relying on my own strength and forgetting that you long to grant us strength and power. Help me draw on your strength today.
—Modified from Psalm 68:35

Confession

Lord, please forgive me for judging other people because of their sins as if my sins aren't that bad. Please forgive me for taking your goodness and patience for granted and forgetting that they are designed to lead me to repentance—not smugness! Please soften my heart that I might see my own sin from your perspective and turn back to you.
—Inspired by Romans 2:3-4

Lord, please forgive us for our many sins. Just like your children of old, we have sinned greatly even though you showered your goodness on us. Help us to live for you. Help our leaders to know and honor you.
—Modified from Nehemiah 9:32-35

Lord, forgive me for allowing jealousy and selfish ambition anywhere near my heart. Help me remember that this "wisdom" is not from you, but is earthly, sensual, and demonic. For where jealousy and selfish ambition are, there is confusion and every evil deed.
—Modified from James 3:14-16

Lord, please forgive us for, unlike you, we can be so quick to anger. Lord, help me remember that a gentle answer turns away wrath, but a harsh word stirs up anger.
—Modified from Proverbs 15:1

Lord, please help us when we, like David, burn with anger against other people's sin. David said to Nathan, "As Yahweh lives, the man who has done this deserves to die!" But he was rebuked when Nathan replied, "You are that man." Help us realize that sometimes the sins that bother us the most are the very ones that we have also committed. Please help us acknowledge our own guilt and confess our sins.

—Modified from 2 Samuel 12:4-10

　　Please forgive me for not allowing your love to flow through me. So often, I am not patient or kind. Forgive me for times when I envy, or brag, or am proud and seek my own way instead of what's better for others.
　　　　　　　　　—Modified from 1 Corinthians 13:4-5

　　Please forgive me, for often my life could not be summarized by "love." Please forgive me for not loving you or loving others the way I should.
　　　　　　　　　—Inspired by 1 John 4:19

　　Lord, when I think of your holiness, I can't help but acknowledge that my sins are many and serious, but I take great comfort in your Word. You are the high and exalted one who is holy and who lives forever in a high and holy place. But you are also with the one who is contrite and humble in spirit, to revive the spirit of the humble and repentant. Lord, I do confess my sins, and I thank you for your forgiveness. Please help me live for you.
　　　　　　　　　—Modified from Isaiah 57:15-16

　　You commanded us to be holy to you; for you are holy, and you have set us apart from the peoples, that we should be yours. Lord, please forgive us for so easily getting distracted from our most important relationship—the one with you. Forgive us for being more concerned about pleasing other people than pleasing you.
　　　　　　　　　—Modified from Leviticus 20:26

　　Lord, please forgive me for turning from you, the God who can save me. I confess I have forgotten the Rock who can hide me. Even though I work hard, I don't have anything to show for it because I have not trusted in you,

but sought help from those who only pretend to have your strength and ability to help.
—Modified from Isaiah 17:10

Lord, please guide me in your truth and teach me, for you are the God of my salvation, I wait for you all day long. O Lord, you are the eternal one. Please do not hold the sins of my youth against me. Remember me according to your loving-kindness for your goodness' sake.
—Modified from Psalm 25:5-7

Lord, please forgive us for just drifting through life so distracted with just getting by. Forgive us for not realizing that the hour has come for us to wake up. For salvation is nearer to us now than when we first believed. So then let us cast off the works of darkness and put on the armor of light. Let us walk properly as in the daytime, not in drunkenness and all kinds of immorality, not in arguing and jealousy. But may we put on the Lord Jesus Christ, and make no provision for the flesh, to gratify its desires.
—Modified from Romans 13:11-14

Lord, please forgive me for lacking humility and jumping at the chance to find fault in others, to complain about or even judge them. Please forgive me for forgetting that you alone are the righteous judge who is able to save and to destroy. Please forgive me for judging other people.
—Modified from James 4:10-12

Time with God

  Lord, please forgive us and heal our land. We've pushed you out of our schools and our public forums. We've exchanged the truth for a lie, and worshiped and served the creature rather than you, our Creator. You have allowed our culture to spiral downward to ever increasing levels of spiritual and moral corruption.
       —Modified from Romans 1:28-32

  Lord, I read in your Word that like so many other kings, Zedekiah did what was evil in your sight even though you were the Lord his God, and he refused to humble himself... Likewise, all the leaders of the priests and the people became more and more unfaithful. Lord, please forgive our leaders—both in the church and in the government—for being unfaithful to you. It is so easy to drift from worshiping and trusting you, to trusting in ourselves or looking for help from others. Lord, please forgive our sins.
      —Modified from 2 Chronicles 36:12-14

  Please forgive me for taking your faithfulness for granted. Please forgive me for my sin and help me to choose the way of escape that you provide rather than the momentary pleasure of sin.
      —Modified from 1 Corinthians 10:13

  Lord, I call out to you; you are my Rock, do not turn a deaf ear to me. For if you remain silent, it would be as if I were already dead. Hear my cry for mercy as I call to you for help, as I lift up my hands in prayer toward your Most Holy Place.
      —Modified from Psalm 28:1-2

  Lord, my sin causes me to despair sometimes; please forgive me for my sin and for doubting your

forgiveness. I know it is because of your amazing love that we are not consumed because your mercies never fail. Indeed, they are new every morning; great is your faithfulness.
—Modified from Lamentations 3:21-23

Lord Jesus, I thank you for being a great high priest, able to sympathize with our weaknesses. For you too were tempted in all things, just like us, but you faced those temptations without yielding to sin. Please forgive me for my sins and help me to live for you.
—Modified from Hebrews 4:14-15

Lord, your Word says we are to be free from the love of money and be satisfied with what we have, for you have promised, "I will in no way leave you, and neither will I in any way forsake you."

Please forgive me for not being content with your love, your presence, and your gifts in my life and for so easily getting distracted—pursuing other things that promise fulfillment.
—Inspired by Hebrews 13:5

Lord, please forgive me for trying to build my life on a foundation other than your commands and precepts. Lord, forgive me for being like the man who hears your words and doesn't do what you've said. It's like building a house without a foundation, against which the stream broke, and immediately it fell, and the ruin of that house was great. Please forgive me for making a mess of things. Please help me build my life on your truths. Only then will I be able to withstand the storms of life.
—Inspired by Luke 6:47-49

Time with God

I confess that I can lose sight of your presence and work in my life and drift into sin. But I take great comfort, Lord, that even though you are the high and holy God, who lives forever, and you live in a high and holy place, I rejoice that you also live with people who are humble and repentant, so that you can restore our confidence and hope.

—Modified from Isaiah 57:15

Lord, I know that we didn't choose you, but you chose us, and appointed us, that we should go and bear fruit, and that our fruit should remain; that whatever we ask you, in the name of your son, Jesus, you already long to give to us. Please forgive me for getting so easily distracted by the cares and worries of this life that I don't bear fruit for you and that I so often look to resolve my challenges in my own "strength" and forget that you, the Almighty God, long for me to bring my needs before you.

—Modified from John 15:16

Lord, you often refer to your relationship with your people in terms of a marriage. You also warn us that the ways of this world are very different from your ways. Lord, please forgive us for being like an unfaithful spouse, being so easily distracted from the simplicity and purity of devotion to Christ.

—Inspired by Isaiah 62:5, John 17:14, 2 Corinthians 11:3

Thanksgiving

Lord, I am so grateful that you, O Lord, are high above all nations, your glory above the heavens. Who is like you, our God, who has his seat on high, and yet you stoop down to see in heaven and in the earth?
—Modified from Psalm 113:4-6

Lord, I am grateful that you are in charge. For you, my Lord, are God of gods and Lord of lords, the great, mighty, and awesome God, who is not partial and takes no bribe. You execute justice for the fatherless and the widow and love the sojourner, giving him food and clothing.
—Modified from Deuteronomy 10:17-18

Lord, I thank you that as the angel told Mary, I know that with you, nothing will be impossible.
—Modified from Luke 1:37

O come, let us sing to the Lord: Let us make a joyful noise to the rock of our salvation. May we come before your presence with thanksgiving, and make a joyful noise to you with songs. For you, Lord, are a great God, and a great King above all gods.
—Modified from Psalm 95:1-3

I am so grateful that you, Lord, reign! You are clothed with majesty and armed with strength. You established the world. It cannot be moved. Your throne is established from long ago. You are from everlasting. Your statutes stand firm. Holiness adorns your house, Yahweh, forevermore.

—Modified from Psalm 93:1-2

Lord, I am so grateful that, since you are eternal, you can declare the end from the beginning and from ancient times things that are still to come.

—Modified from Isaiah 46:10

Lord, I thank you that although there are many things that are impossible for mankind, we can rejoice that with you all things are possible.

—Modified from Matthew 19:26

Thank you, Lord. I have tasted and seen that You, Yahweh, are indeed good. I am truly blessed because I take refuge in you.

—Modified from Psalm 34:8

Lord I give thanks to you, for you are good, for your loving-kindness endures forever.

—Modified from Psalm 118:1

O, Lord, I thank you for your law. How I love it! It is my meditation all day.

Your commandments make me wiser than my enemies, for your commandments are always with me.

I have more understanding than all my teachers, for your testimonies are my meditation.

—Modified from Psalm 119:97-101

Thanksgiving

Lord, I thank you for your amazing patience as you waited for me to understand your gospel and repent from my own sins.
—Modified from 2 Peter 3:9

Lord, I thank you for the Holy Spirit, who is continually working in my life to develop patience in me (along with the other fruit of the Spirit).
—Modified from Galatians 5:22-25

Lord Jesus, I thank you that you demonstrated your own love for us in this: While we were still sinners, you died for us.
—Modified from Romans 5:8

Lord, I thank you for how great a love you have given to us, that we should be called children of God!
—Modified from 1 John 3:1

Lord, I am grateful for your holiness. For there is no one as holy as you, Yahweh, for there is no one besides you, nor is there any rock like our God.
—Modified from 1 Samuel 2:2

Lord, we rejoice with thankfulness, for you, the mighty one, have done great things for us. Holy is your name.
—Modified from Luke 1:49

Lord, I thank you that you alone are my rock and my salvation, my fortress. I will not be shaken.
—Modified from Psalm 62:6

Lord, my days are as brief as a long shadow as the sun goes down. It will soon vanish like withered grass. But I am thankful that you, Yahweh, are enthroned forever; your renown endures to all generations.
—Modified from Psalm 102:11-12

Heavenly Father, I thank you for you made us fit to be partakers of the inheritance of the saints in light; you delivered us out of the power of darkness, and translated us into the Kingdom of the Son you love, in whom we have our redemption, the forgiveness of our sins. Hallelujah!
—Modified from Colossians 1:12-14

Lord, I thank you for not abandoning us in your wrath, but rather you loved us so much that you gave your one and only Son, that whoever believes in him should not perish, but have eternal life. For you didn't send your Son into the world to judge the world, but that the world should be saved through him.
—Modified from John 3:16-17

Father God, I thank you for the new life you have given us. Even though we were dead in transgressions and sins, you, being rich in love and mercy, made us alive together with Christ. Lord, I know it is by grace we have been saved. Lord, not only did you make us alive with your Son, but you raised us up with him, and made us to sit with him in the heavenly places in Christ Jesus.
—Modified from Ephesians 2:1-6

Lord, I thank you that you are faithful and will not allow us to be tempted above what we are able, but with the temptation will also provide the way of escape, that we may be able to endure it. Lord, I also thank you that when we neglect to use the "way of escape" that you had provided and stumble into sin, that you still remain faithful. For you have promised if we confess our sins, you are faithful and righteous to forgive our sins, and to cleanse us from all unrighteousness.

—Modified from 1 Corinthians 10:13 and 1 John 1:9

Dear God, I rejoice in your faithfulness. I know that you are not a man, that you should lie, nor the son of man, that you should repent. Have you said something, and will you not do it? Or have you spoken, and will you not make it good?

—Modified from Numbers 23:19

Lord, I proclaim that you alone are my rock. Lord, I thank you that by your grace, we, like living stones, are being built up as a spiritual house, to be a holy priesthood, to offer up spiritual sacrifices acceptable to you through Jesus Christ. By your grace, we are a chosen race, a royal priesthood, a holy nation, a people for your own possession, Lord, so that we may proclaim that you are the one who called us out of darkness into your marvelous light.

—Modified from 1 Peter 2:1-10

Lord, I am so grateful that even though we were once far from you, you showed us your mercy. We were foolish, disobedient, deceived, and enslaved by various desires and "pleasures," living in malice and envy—hating and being hated. But you saved us, not because of any "good works" that we had done, but because of your mercy, you saved us through the work of the Holy Spirit cleansing us and giving us new life.

—Modified from Titus 3:3-5

Lord, I am so thankful that you are merciful, especially when I remember that I was spiritually dead in my own transgressions and sins. But, because you are so rich in mercy, and you loved us so much, you made us alive, together with your Son, Jesus. That would have been more than enough. But you even raised us and seated us in heavenly places in Christ Jesus.
—Modified from Ephesians 2:4-6

What great nation is there that has a god so near to it as is the LORD our God whenever we call on Him? Lord, I thank you that you are near and that you invite us to call on you.
—Modified from Deuteronomy 4:7

Lord, I thank you that you hear my cry, dear God, and that you listen to my prayer. From the end of the earth, I will call to you, when my heart is overwhelmed. Lead me to the rock that is higher than I. For you have been a refuge for me, a strong tower from the enemy. I will dwell in your tent forever. I will take refuge in the shelter of your wings.
—Modified from Psalm 61:1-4

Lord, I thank you that you are not limited by any boundaries. I rejoice that you are a God close by and far off also—you fill heaven and earth!
—Modified from Jeremiah 23:23-24

You said to Jacob, "I am El-Shaddai—God Almighty. Be fruitful and multiply. You will become a great nation, even many nations. Kings will be among your descendants!" Lord, I thank you for fulfilling your promise. You are indeed almighty and faithful.
—Modified from Genesis 35:11

Thanksgiving

Lord, I am so thankful that your faithful love never ends! Your mercies never cease. It is by your mercies, O Lord, that we are not consumed, because your compassions fail not. They are new every morning: Great is your faithfulness.

—Modified from Lamentations 3:22-23

Supplication

Lord, I know you commanded us to "Go, and make disciples of all nations, baptizing them and teaching them..." But, Lord, my favorite part is that you also reminded us that you are with us always, even to the end of the age. Lord, please help us to be faithful in partnering with you in sharing the gospel. Amen!
—Modified from Matthew 28:18-20

Lord, by your Holy Spirit, please help us worship and bow down: Let us kneel before you, Lord, our maker. For you are our God, and we are the people of your pasture and the sheep of your hand. Lord, today if we hear your voice, please give us willing and obedient hearts to serve you with all our heart.
—Modified from Psalm 95:6-7

Lord, by your grace and through the work of your Holy Spirit, may I truly know and take this to heart this day. You, LORD, are God in heaven above and on the earth below. There is no other. May you truly be the Lord of my life today.

—Modified from Deuteronomy 4:39

Lord, may I like Rahab of Jericho recognize and proclaim that you are God in the heavens above and on the earth beneath.

—Modified from Joshua 2:11

Lord, you are God, and there is no other. I know that you are God, and there is none like you. You declare the end from the beginning, and from ancient times things that are not yet done. Please guide us in your ways.

—Modified from Isaiah 46:9-10

Lord, you see the end from the beginning. Please give me your perspective. I lift up my soul to you, O Lord. O my God, in you I trust. Show me your ways, O LORD, teach me your paths; guide me in your truth and teach me, for you are God my Savior. Please help me to trust in you all day long.

—Modified from Psalm 25:1-5

Lord, I thank you that although there are many things that are impossible for mankind, we can rejoice that with you all things are possible.

—Modified from Matthew 19:26

Thank you, Lord. I have tasted and seen that You, Yahweh, are indeed good. I am truly blessed because I take refuge in you.

—Modified from Psalm 34:8

Lord I give thanks to you, for you are good, for your loving-kindness endures forever.

—Modified from Psalm 118:1

O, Lord, I thank you for your law. How I love it! It is my meditation all day.

Your commandments make me wiser than my enemies, for your commandments are always with me.

I have more understanding than all my teachers, for your testimonies are my meditation.
—Modified from Psalm 119:97-101

Lord, your Word tells us that "The fear of God is the beginning of knowledge, but the foolish despise wisdom and instruction." Lord, please help me to always give you the place of honor and respect you deserve in my life.
—Modified from Proverbs 1:7

Lord, help me remember that a fool vents all of his anger, but a wise man brings himself under control. And that one who is slow to anger is better than the mighty; one who rules his own spirit is better than he who takes a city.
—Modified from Proverbs 16:32, 29:11

Lord, help me remember that whoever is patient and slow to anger shows great understanding, but whoever has a quick temper highlights his foolishness.
—Modified from Proverbs 14:29

Lord, please help us remember that you are our God and that you are the only God. Help us to love you as we should—with all our heart, with all our soul, with all our mind, and with all our strength. Also, please help us to love others as you would.
—Modified from Mark 12:29-30

Lord, remembering that we have the confidence to enter the Most Holy Place by the blood of Jesus and that we have a great priest over the house of God, please help us draw near to you with a sincere heart and with the full assurance that faith brings. And Lord, the next time we attend any small group meeting or even a worship service, please show us how we can pass on your love to others by encouraging at least one person there.

—Modified from Hebrews 10:19-22

Lord, please help me ascribe to you glory and strength...ascribe to you, O LORD, the glory due your name. May I worship you in the wonder of your holiness.

—Modified from Psalm 29:1-2

Lord, our culture is so obsessed with sex; please give us your perspective. Please help us remember that your will for us is that we set ourselves apart and live holy lives. Lord, teach us how to take charge of our own bodies, maintaining purity and honor. May we not give in to the passion of lust or take advantage of anyone this way.

—Modified from 1 Thessalonians 4:3-8

Lord, please help me not to give in to fear, or to be afraid. Help me remember that you declared it to us long ago, and have shown it. Lord, we are your witnesses. Is there a God besides you? Indeed, there is not. I don't know any other Rock.

—Modified from Isaiah 44:8

Lord God, you are our God forever and ever. Please be our guide as long as we live.

—Modified from Psalm 48:14

Lord, please help me receive your words of wisdom and store up your commands within me. May your wisdom and understanding keep me and deliver me from the way of evil, from those who speak perverse things and forsake the paths of uprightness to walk in the ways of darkness, who rejoice to do evil and delight in the perverseness of evil. Lord, please allow your light to help me see through their schemes.

—Modified from Proverbs 2:1, 10-14

Lord, I think of the Apostle Paul toward the end of his years on earth saying, "I have fought the good fight. I have finished the course. I have kept the faith" and knowing that he would receive a crown of righteousness from you, the Righteous Judge. Lord, please help me live my life today in such a way that I would look forward to the Day of Judgment when you appear.

—Modified from 2 Timothy 4:7-8

Heavenly Father, you have told us that you love the Son and have given all things into his hand. I know that whoever believes in the Son has eternal life; whoever does not obey the Son shall not see life, but the wrath of God remains on him. Lord, please help me understand the seriousness and the urgency of introducing people to your Son. Please guide me and empower me by your Holy Spirit that I may know how to share the gospel with clarity, love, gentleness, respect, and boldness.

—Inspired by John 3:35-36; Colossians 4:4; Ephesians 6:20; 1 Peter 3:15

Lord, may I be like Sarah, who even though she initially laughed at the thought of having a child in her old age, knew that you were faithful and would keep your promise. May I be able to trust your faithfulness to do what you have promised even though I may not understand how.

—Modified from Genesis 18:9-15 and Hebrews 11:11

Dear God, I rejoice in your faithfulness. I know that you are not a man, that you should lie, nor the son of man, that you should repent. Have you said something, and will you not do it? Or have you spoken, and will you not make it good?

—Modified from Numbers 23:19

Lord, help us to not be worried about the future. Help us to trust you knowing that you are faithful. Lord, as the God of peace, may you sanctify us completely. May our whole spirit, soul, and body be preserved blameless at the coming of your Son, our Lord Jesus Christ.

—Modified from 1 Thessalonians 5:23-24

May the words of my mouth and the meditation of my heart be pleasing to you, O Lord, my rock, and my redeemer.

—Modified from Psalm 19:14

Lord, please help us to have right priorities. Lord, you have shown us what is good. What do you, Yahweh, require of us, but to act justly, to love mercy, and to walk humbly with our God. Realizing how mercy is such a part of who you are, please help me this day to love people by showing mercy to those you put in my path.

—Inspired by Micah 6:8

Lord, we know that you are a God of mercy; please help us come boldly to your throne of grace, that we may receive mercy in our times of need.

—Modified from Hebrews 4:16

Lord, you have promised that when the righteous cry, you hear and deliver them out of all their anguish. You are near to those who are discouraged and have lost all

hope. Please help me be aware of your presence and comfort in my life today.
—Modified from Psalm 34:17-18

Lord, please help us remember we don't belong in this world. Help us resist those desires of the flesh that battle against our soul. May we live lives of integrity among the people so that, even when some may be inclined to call us evildoers, they see our good works and might give glory to you when you return.
—Modified from 1 Peter 2:11-12

Lord, you have promised that where two or three are gathered together in your name, you are present among them. Lord, when we meet for worship, with our small group or even with some friends for dinner, please help us be aware that you are right there with us.
—Modified from Matthew 18:20

Lord, I want to praise you as I should. Please help me make a joyful shout to you! Help me sing to the glory of your name! Help me proclaim, "How awesome are your deeds! Through the greatness of your power, your enemies submit themselves to you. All the earth will worship you, and will sing to you; they will sing to your name."
—Modified from Psalm 66:1-4

Lord, seeing how faithful you are by your very nature, please help me to be faithful to you and to those around me. Lord, please help me to be faithful in the very little, that you may be able to trust me with greater responsibilities.
—Inspired by Luke 16:10-12

References

Endnotes

1. Excerpted from *If God Should Speak* by Clyde Herring, quoted in LeFever, Marlene D. *Creative Teaching Methods*. Colorado Springs, Colorado: Cook Ministry Resources, 1996. 73. Print.

Cover Photo

Cover Photo credit: PEARL, photo ID: 248303, www.Lighthouse.com

Scripture Translations Used

All Scripture paraphrases are those of the author unless otherwise noted.

NIV: Scripture quotations marked (NIV) are taken from the Holy Bible, New International Version®, NIV®.

Copyright © 1973, 1978, 1984, 2011 by Biblica, Inc.™ Used by permission of Zondervan. All rights reserved worldwide. www.zondervan.com The "NIV" and "New International Version" are trademarks registered in the United States Patent and Trademark Office by Biblica, Inc.™

NKJV: Scripture quotations marked (NKJV) are taken from the New King James Version®. Copyright © 1982 by Thomas Nelson, Inc. Used by permission. All rights reserved.

NLT: Scripture quotations marked (NLT) are taken from the Holy Bible, New Living Translation, copyright © 1996, 2004, 2007 by Tyndale House Foundation. Used by permission of Tyndale House Publishers, Inc., Carol Stream, Illinois 60188. All rights reserved.

VOICE: Scripture quotations marked (VOICE) are taken from taken from The Voice™. Copyright © 2008 by Ecclesia Bible Society. Used by permission. All rights reserved.

WEB: Verses marked (WEB) are from the World English Bible (WEB), a public domain (no copyright) Modern English translation of the Holy Bible, based on the American Standard Version of the Holy Bible first published in 1901.

Acknowledgements

I'd like to acknowledge that the input of many people has made this book possible.

I am especially grateful for the many people who have encouraged, stimulated, or tolerated me through the many conversations about and versions of this book. Among the many people in this category, I would especially like to thank my wife, Alesa, my adult children (Cathy, Grace, and John) for their patience and encouragement along this journey.

I am grateful for the many staff and faculty of International Teams, Moody Bible Institute, and Bethel Seminary of the East for all they poured into me throughout my education. They helped me stay focused on God and grow in my relationship with and effectiveness for him. I am especially appreciative of Dr. Ron Sauer, Dr.

Brian Labosier, Dr. Wayne Hansen, and the many other faculty members who encouraged and equipped me to study the Scriptures, theology, and the biblical languages. Without their help, I would not have even begun a project like this.

I am also grateful for the support of so many who made it possible for me to graduate from Bible college and seminary without student loans. Among them are Dennis and Rose Cunningham, Jim and Lupita Cunningham, Joe and Rose DeRuvo, and Alan and Jennie Kingsbury.

Margo Grant, Steve Treash, Kevin Harney, Dan Kimball, Jeff Goins, Jim Woods, John C. Maxwell, Michael Hyatt, Charlie Wetzel, Kelly O'Dell Stanley, and Jon Acuff have also served as great examples and sources of encouragement as I began and continue to learn the craft and business of writing.

About the Author

Kevin T. Cunningham

Rock and roll was my life! I was a disc jockey on radio and in nightclubs. I used to entertain people for a night; now I can impact people for eternity.

Serving God has included Christian radio; church planting in Milan, Italy; and local pastoral ministry in the U.S. in Indiana, Connecticut, and New Hampshire. I am currently serving as Intentional Interim Minister for a church in Lynn, Massachusetts. The fuller version of my faith story is included below.

Websites

www.TimeWithGodBook.com
> for more updates and additional downloadable resources.

www.EncourageAndEquip.com
> for more resources designed to help you grow in your faith.

www.PastorKevin.net
> for speaking, consulting, and pulpit supply.

Coming in late 2016 or early 2017:

www.CloseTheBackDoor.net
> for articles, training resources, and discussions to help your church welcome and assimilate newcomers into your church.

Faith Story

Rock and roll was my life and my god. When I was 8 years old, I remember very clearly wanting to sing or play the drums. When I was 12, I learned that I would never make a dime doing either one. So, I set my sights on radio. I was imitating DJs by 13 and by the age of 17 was on the air. I also worked as a disc jockey in nightclubs and at private parties and served as emcee for many 1950s acts such as Bobby Rydell, the Drifters, the Five Satins, the Coasters, and the Angels. Born in New York City, I attended Roman Catholic schools through high school. Although my level of participation varied, I had always enjoyed a sense of God's existence and of his protection over my life.

Through the invitation of a Christian friend, I started attending a Bible-teaching church. I marveled at how the people actually seemed happy to be there. I also heard them talk about Jesus in a way that I had never heard before. I remember being puzzled, thinking there are so many different religions and churches, how can I know which one is right? I was taught from the cradle that the

Bible was the Word of God and that Jesus was the Son of God. So, I bought a Bible to see what Jesus had to say. (During this time I would talk with a believing friend, listen to a fair amount of Christian radio, and attend a Catholic church in the morning and an evangelical church in the evening.) It was about nine months of reading the gospels twice through before the message took.

I was struck by Jesus' perfection in all he did. I was most amazed at how he related with people, especially those who were trying to harm him. In the light of his standard, I realized for the first time that I fell far short. I was getting a handle by now on heaven and hell and the frightening realization that I was heading in the wrong direction. Only then could I really understand the fact that Jesus not only died for the sins of the world, but he also died for my sins! I accepted, by faith, the fact that his blood was shed in my place to set me free.

There followed another nine months of struggle, trying to reconcile my rock music career with my newfound faith and praying to know God's will for my life. It was not until I made a clear break with all my former ways of earning a living and trusted totally in the Lord that God was able to break through with clear guidance. On Christmas Eve of 1982, I loaded up my music inventory of 500 albums and 1,000 singles in the car and dropped them in a big green dumpster. Not that the music itself was all that bad. I knew it was something I needed to do. Somehow, I knew it was time to allow Jesus the opportunity to guide my life.

After that crisis moment, it only took two and a half weeks to learn of a position in Christian radio and send a tape, and my belongings were in the back of the car on the way to Kentucky and WNKJ.

I was very content working in Christian broadcasting with a great team and an excellent format. Little did I know, it was just the beginning. God would then lead me to serve him in church planting missions in Milan, Italy and pastoral ministry in Connecticut, Indiana, and New Hampshire. As of this writing, I am serving as an Intentional Interim Pastor in Lynn, Massachusetts.

The journey continues.

—Kevin T. Cunningham